The Novels of Roger Vailland

American University Studies

Series II
Romance Languages and Literature

Vol. 48

PETER LANG
New York · Berne · Frankfurt am Main

Jo Ann McNatt

The Novels of Roger Vailland

The Amateur and the Professional

PETER LANG
New York · Berne · Frankfurt am Main

Library of Congress Cataloging in Publication Data

McNatt, Jo Ann:

The Novels of Roger Vailland.

(American University Studies. Series II. Romance Languages and Literature ; vol. 48)
Bibliography: p.
Includes Index.
1. Vailland, Roger--Fictional works. 2. Amateurism in literature. 3. Occupations in literature. 4. Authors in literature. I. Title. II. Series.
PQ2643.A136Z74 1986 843'.914 86-2965
ISBN 0-8204-0336-9
ISSN 0740-9257

CIP-Kurztitelaufnahme der Deutschen Bibliothek

McNatt, Jo Ann:
The Novels of Roger Vailland : The Amateur and the Professional / Jo Ann McNatt. - New York ; Berne ; Frankfurt am Main : Lang, 1986.
(American University Studies : Ser. 2, Romance Languages and Literature ; Vol. 48)
ISBN 0-8204-0336-9
NE: American University Studies / 02

Printed by Weihert-Druck GmbH, Darmstadt (West-Germany)

ACKNOWLEDGEMENTS

For their encouragement and advice through the years I would like to express appreciation to Professors Harry Stewart of Clemson University and Stirling Haig, George Daniel, and Edouard Morot-Sir of the University of North Carolina at Chapel Hill. For their time and effort on my behalf I thank the staff of the Clemson University Computer Center--especially Sandi Piazza, whose expertise and patience were essential to this project, and Jay Crawford, who gave much advice in times of emergency.

TABLE OF CONTENTS

INTRODUCTION

Since his death in 1965, and particularly since the publication of his *Écrits Intimes* in 1968 and *Lettres à sa famille* in 1972, Roger Vailland has been the object of increasing interest among scholars and the general public. As recently as 1984 René Ballet edited a new collection of Vailland's pre-war newspaper articles in *Chronique des années folles à la libération 1928-1945*. Most of the other work on Vailland has used the biography of the man, the *Écrits Intimes*, his essays, plays, and novels for purposes of mutual elucidation. Among books devoted to him must be mentioned *Les Saisons de Roger Vailland* by François Bott and *Roger Vailland, tentative de description* by Jean-Jacques Brochier, both published in 1969 and both mainly concerned with the man and his life as seen through the works; *Entretiens: Roger Vailland*, published in 1970 under the direction of Max Chaleil, containing unpublished texts by Vailland himself and articles giving personal views of the man and the work written by members of his family, friends, and critics. Among more scholarly approaches are *Esquisse pour la psychanalyse d'un libertin* by Jean Recanati, published in 1971, and *Libertinage et tragique dans l'oeuvre de Roger Vailland* by Michel Picard, published in 1972. The latter is a masterful work, classifying the characters in Vailland's novels and plays from the standpoint of Freudian psychology. *Roger Vailland: un écrivain au service du peuple* by Jean-Pierre Tusseau, published in 1976, contains some solid ideas, but is marred from a scholarly standpoint by quotations from Vailland's novels presented in the text with no indications that they are quotations. The only substantive work to date in English on Vailland is *Roger Vailland, The Man and His Masks* by J. E.

Flower, published in 1975. This book furnishes an excellent introduction of Vailland and his writing to the English-speaking reader and follows for the works what seems to be the most sensible approach, considering them in the order in which they were written and published.

On many occasions Roger Vailland defined himself as a "libertin." In his essay "Quelques Réflexions sur la singularité d'être français" he writes that what is essentially French can be defined "avec toutes les locutions qui ont _libre_ pour racine, à condition de n'en exclure aucune: liberté, esprit-libre, libre-penseur et également libertinage" (_Le Regard Froid_ 17). He defines the latter as "l'art du plaisir pratiqué par un esprit libre" (20). In the same essay he defines the amateur:

> "Amateur" a une double signification.
>
> D'une part, c'est celui qui aime et qui _s'y connaît_. Cela implique science, goût et plaisir exquis tiré de la science et du goût. . . .
>
> L'amateur d'autre part c'est celui qui ne fait pas profession. Il n'est pas contraint par la nécessité. C'est volontairement qu'il s'abandonne à son goût et il ne cesse jamais de le dominer.
>
> À ce dernier sens, nous retrouvons l'opposition cartésienne entre _l'action_ et la _passion_. L'amateur n'est pas la victime, l'objet d'une passion, il n'est pas _agi_, il sait en toute occasion rester le sujet qui agit; c'est la définition même de la vertu. (22)

This essay is dated 11-12 June 1945. Vailland's first novel had been written the preceding summer, when the author was thirty-six years old. In the next twenty years he wrote eight other novels, in all of which can be seen the ideas and problems introduced in this essay and in the first novel.

It is obvious from the definitions above that the _amateur_ and the _libertin_ are the same kind of person. The first part of the definition explains the art of pleasure and the second part the "esprit libre." The wording makes clear that _profession_ is understood in the sense of a profession of faith or love, as an absolute commitment which is in conflict with the concept of the "esprit libre." Seeing oneself as a "libertin," especially in the context of Cartesian "vertu," connotes the possibility of willfully and rationally defining oneself and of trying to live by this definition; it implies a process of self-creation and self-criticism involving a necessary division of the self into actor and spectator. It also implies a willed artificiality, as opposed to what is natural and spontaneous. Choosing "libertin" as a self-definition in the eighteenth-century context in which Vailland uses it implies, in addition to the artificiality, an aristocratic, elitist position, represented in Vailland's pantheon by Sade and Valmont. The art of pleasure or the art of writing for pleasure as an amateur requires a certain amount of time and resources available to be devoted to it, as seen in Laclos, Valéry-Larbaud, or Gobineau; in his introduction to the Livre de Poche edition of Les Pléïades Vailland describes Gobineau as an "amateur éclairé" (Gobineau 5).

The possibility and desirability of living a self-definition and of being an amateur in the middle of the twentieth century in the "real" world of love, sex, marriage, money, and politics are the themes explored in the novels of Roger Vailland. All the novels, but especially the first four, involve a search for personal identity, or for happiness, usually expressed in terms of a meaningful task to be done, or financial independence, or both. The characters are faced with the constraints of family and society and the necessities of financial security in conflict with the need to be "un esprit libre" and to experience pleasure. There are continual comparisons, by analogy or contrast, between human beings, faced with these conflicts, and plants and animals, which are free to develop according to their natures, but which, because of this very fact, fall easy prey to the "esprit libre."

In 1951, after the publication of the first four novels, Vailland returned once more to the amateur-professional dichotomy in an essay entitled "De l'Amateur" (*Le Regard froid* 111-132). In this essay he calls himself a "faiseur de livres" and compares art, not to be confused with Art, to sports and the dance. He divides artists, cyclists, and dancers into three groups: the *en amateur*, who actually does whatever is involved in the art; the professional, who is chosen from the best of the *en amateurs*; and the *amateur*, who was at one time an *en amateur*, but for one reason or another did not become a professional. It is the amateur who actually judges and supports the *en amateur* and the professional, who is thus the champion, the hero. In the introduction to *Les Pléïades* mentioned above, Vailland, after listing Gobineau's many accomplishments as an amateur before the publication of *Les Pléïades*, writes: "Il n'avait encore excellé que dans l'amitié" (5). The professional, on the other hand, has proved his excellence before an audience of *en amateurs* and of *amateurs*.

In Vailland's writing the novelist as a professional becomes increasingly important. *La Fête*, his penultimate novel, is a description of a novelist who is writing a novel. The author as a character in the novel is a feature that becomes more prominent. Of the last five novels, three are written in the first person by an author-narrator who participates to varying degrees in the action of the novels, culminating in *La Truite*, the last novel, where the narrator begins to look at the other people in the novel as characters and says: "Je commençais de les envisager sous l'angle du professionnel" (79). The novels record the twenty-year journey from the view of the professional as the antithesis of the "esprit libre" to this public assumption of profession and show to what extent Vailland succeeded in finding in the novelist the synthesis of the "libertin," the amateur, the professional, the hero, and the champion.

THE MIDDLE-CLASS SEARCH FOR PLACE

Vailland's first four novels are written in the third person by an omniscient narrator, they have protagonists who are the same age as Vailland at the time depicted in the novels, and they concern characters with a middle-class background such as Vailland's trying to live with other people and to find a place for themselves in the world. The first novel, *Drôle de Jeu*, was written during World War II while Vailland was cut off from his Resistance group. At the time he was already in his late thirties, and the ideas and problems which concerned him did not basically change from then until the end of his life. Changing attitudes toward the ideas and changing solutions to the problems occasioned by changing conditions are reflected in the later novels. The themes of all the later novels can be seen in *Drôle de Jeu*; thus it is necessary to study rather carefully this first novel. (An earlier novel, *Un Homme du peuple sous la Révolution*, was written in collaboration with Raymond Manevy and published in *Le Peuple* in 1937. It was published again in 1947 by Corrêa and appears in vol. 10 of the *Oeuvres Complètes*.)

Drôle de Jeu is the story of Marat (the *nom de guerre* of a Resistance leader in a communications unit) during a period of about a month from the end of March to the end of April 1944. Through interior monologues and excerpts from an earlier journal kept by Marat, then François Lamballe, the period extends back ten or fifteen years. The novel is divided into five *Journées*, all except the third taking place in Paris. The novel is a portrayal of the daily life and dangers of a Resistance group, who are all amateurs because "les professionnels du patriotisme" (83) have gone over to the side of the enemy.

The novel also depicts other segments of society in occupied France, such as black-marketeers, collaborationist journalists, minor functionaries, peasants, members of the provincial middle-class. However, the novel for the most part follows Marat; it is his view of and relation to these different milieux which constitute the novel. Aside from the everyday dangers and pleasures such as the sabotage of a German train in the country and Marat's seduction of Annie, the actual plot revolves around Marat's former lover Mathilde and her efforts to free her present lover Dani from a German prison. Marat does not trust her, but Rodrigue and Frédéric, two young Communists, are dazzled by her worldliness. She succeeds in finding out about a rendez-vous of group leaders and informs the Germans, who set a trap for them. Marat, by chance association and deductive reasoning, realizes that the trap has been set and succeeds in warning all except Frédéric, who is captured.

The straightforward third-person recital of events, the daily comings and goings of the members of the Resistance, are interspersed with the monologues of Marat, excerpts from his journal, and long discussions with other characters on love, politics, philosophy, and money. Liberal use of the _style indirect libre_ makes it difficult, if not impossible, to distinguish between Marat and the narrator. It is the detailed description of the _persona_ Marat-Lamballe as he defines himself to himself, to the other characters, and to the reader which constitutes the primary focus of the novel. The novel situates this _persona_ philosophically, historically, and personally in relation to a specific time, place, and set of circumstances, and it is this _persona_ and the contradictions inherent in it which will form the basis of the later novels.

François is the name by which Vailland was known among his pre-war friends; Lamballe, grandson of Louis XIV, was the son of the illegitimate, but recognized, son of the great king. Thus the pre-war self is seen as a prince, biologically perhaps fit to be king, but without the possibility or necessity of being king. Marat, Vailland's own nom de guerre, was, of course, the fiery revolutionary leader, "l'ami du peuple," whose aim was to destroy the very concept of royalty. The name of the character thus presents his situation and his problem, which are made more explicit by a discussion between him and Rodrigue as to who they would have been if they had lived during the French Revolution. Marat says that he could not have been Napoleon, who at his age was already emperor: "Moi, dans dix ans, je ferai terriblement Ancien Régime . . . passé bien entendu à la Révolution, mieux: artisan de la Révolution, mais Ancien Régime quand même . . . on n'a pas eu impunément vingt ans en 1928" (162). He is not Lamballe, who decided one day to become Marat; rather, he is Lamballe and Marat at the same time. In a discussion with Annie he defines life: " . . . la vie, n'est-ce pas? dans son essence, dans ce qu'elle a de foncièrement angoissant peut être définie comme la liberté de choisir" (269). The novel explores the limits within which one is free to choose and opts for life with its anguish in opposition to forms of "non-life" which are presented as alternatives.

Mathilde tells Marat that Rodrigue has given him the nickname: "Monsieur Plus-rien-ne-m'étonne-le-ciel-m'est-tombé-sur-la-tête-dans-un-bordel-de Tombouctou-en-1789" (320). This nickname presents him rather accurately as someone who has experienced life and learned from these experiences, but who is now older than those with whom he lives and works. He sees himself as a person who has "cette fermeté que les meilleurs de ma génération n'ont acquise qu'après avoir pendant des années, longuement, patiemment, loyalement surmonté une à une toutes leurs contradictions" (23), who is now approaching "la maturité" (60). He can understand those, like Rodrigue and Annie, whose growth has not yet reached this stage of maturity, those like Mathilde, who refuse to face their contradictions, and those like Frédéric, who refuse to grow or face their inner conflicts.

Throughout the novel Marat is constantly aware of the concrete determinations of heredity, environment, and cultural influences. He speaks of his "bonne race montagnarde" (63) and says of Elvire: "Elle est de bonne race" (347). He concludes that Chloé's "intelligence rapide et tout instinctive des êtres et des situations, son aisance à se mouvoir dans les milieux les plus divers, parmi les événements les plus imprévus, tout en restant elle-même" (307-8) come from her Parisian background. He verifies the influence of the immediate sensory environment on his subconscious revery while riding the metro: "C'est drôle, je fais du genou à cette femme, mais je n'ai pas encore 'vu' qu'elle était assise en face de moi" (31). He is aware of the influence of external nature on his moods: "Il avait surtout apprécié le calme d'un pays sans envolées. La montagne l'exaltait . . ." (217-18). Marat's landlady, who is anticlerical by family tradition (117), and Frédéric, who, according to Rodrigue, became a Communist "pour s'affirmer contre le milieu familial" (169), illustrate the influence of the family as do the emotional blackmail used against Annie by her family and the financial blackmail used against Mathilde by hers. Marat is aware of the influence on him of his schooling, which, according to him, taught him a scorn for reason and logic, a scorn which he, unlike others of his generation, has now overcome. He can understand rationally how his contemporaries could embrace fascism: " . . . la révolte, si elle ne s'intègre dans une conscience de classe, mène aussi bien au fascisme qu'au communisme" (29). He sees cultural influences at play in the field of international relations and diplomacy, where statesmen, because of "leur formation, la forme de leur pensée, la nature même de leur être et les qualités qui les firent réussir dans leur pays" (340), are incapable of understanding what is going on in other countries.

He can see these cultural forces at work in himself and in others: "Je n'ai pas le style communiste. Je suis fils de bourgeois. Je lutte contre ma classe de toutes mes forces, mais j'ai hérité de ses vices, j'aime son luxe, ses plaisirs. Beaucoup de choses que le militant ne soupçonne même pas tiennent une grande place dans ma vie" (288). He sees the same kind of influence in Rodrigue's superstitious attitude toward money: "la survivance, intolérable chez des révolutionnaires, du sentiment de sacré, associé à la possession des richesses" (301). Marat is aware that his vices and love of luxury and pleasures are inherited from his background and is not ashamed of them, while the young militant is ashamed because of taboos of a society he does not believe in and wishes to have no part in. Marat realizes the importance of the generational differences between him and his young colleagues. Rodrigue did not go through the years of soul searching which he has experienced, but went directly from the lycée to the battle, forced to "prendre parti" immediately. He realizes that Caracalla, his superior in the Resistance, knows nothing about Parisian nightlife because in 1939 he was only nineteen years old.

When Annie is troubled by the seeming gratuity of her choice of Communism while a girl she knows with the same kind of background as hers and the same style of dress and make-up as hers chose collaboration, Marat realizes that many conscious and unconscious factors influenced Annie's decision: "Supposer qu'elle aurait pu faire un autre choix c'est supposer qu'elle aurait pu naître hottentote; évidemment, mais ce ne serait plus elle; ce genre de questions relève d'un 'usage illégitime de la Raison pure'" (276). When Rodrigue takes Marat to task for the way he behaves with women, the narrator writes that Marat "avait discerné un peu de jalousie, mais aussi un sentiment exact de son appartenance à un milieu, à une époque déjà périmée. Tant pis: _I am what I am_" (311). The two examples of Thucydides, the mercenary who performs "executions" for the group, and who is described by Marat as "foncièrement amoral ou plutôt persuadé que ce qu'il fait est bien _parce que c'est lui qui le fait_" (392), and of the worker who in 1938 told the director of his factory that he was going on strike because: "Ma morale à moi, c'est de ne pas venir demain" (286) illustrate the dangers and advantages of such an acceptance of self. It is evident, however, that Marat's position is one based on lucidity in viewing himself and on a certain acceptance of history and of concrete reality.

His position is contrasted with that of Frédéric, who, according to Annie, is afraid of life, knows nothing written after 1880, and whose every effort "tend à se désincarner" (267):

> Il se regarde du point de vue de Sirius. De là-haut, il n'est plus Frédé X., né en 1922, à Passy, de tel père et de telle mère, myope, asthmatique, les cheveux noirs, vingt-deux dents, licencié, etc. Il échappe aux déterminations concrètes, il n'est plus qu'un homme, l'homme éternel. Homme il doit se conduire de telle manière que tout autre homme à sa place. (268)

Marat, on the other hand, is aware of being a survivor of another time, which he can now look back on and, to a certain extent, understand. He looks upon his life between the ages of twenty and thirty-six as a kind of prolongation of his studies, during which he had refused to "faire carrière" and thus bind himself to a society which he judged outmoded, derisory, and unlikely to survive (163). His boyhood friends were all exposed to the same influences in society and in school as he. His friend, Roger, who died of tetanus from giving himself injections of laudanum, had prophesied at age fifteen that he would commit suicide slowly by taking drugs. Marat concludes: "Il est resté jusqu'à la fin tel qu'il était au sortir du lycée" (25), while Marat has been able to change and adapt to change, in part simply by surviving into another time with its own style and tone. Speaking of the reaction he and his friends had to the suicide of René Crevel, he says: "Une aussi parfaite 'seyance' aussi immédiatement saisie par un groupe donné, à un moment donné, est éminemment significative: toute l'histoire de l'époque peut s'en déduire" (27). Of the experience of the French people, he says: "Les hommes réagissent selon le style de leur époque; en 40 il était caractérisé par la valse musette et le 'cabanon' marseillais; en 44, il s'est haussé jusqu'à la tragédie; nous voici tous devenus personnages de Corneille" (88). He tells Annie that he did not invent the scenario, which was given, that he only put himself "dans le ton" (256). He is able to do this because he has no "situation, famille, foyer" to bind him: "Toute sa vie était dans l'avenir" (162).

This refusal to be bound allows him more freedom of movement and of choice and gives him the capability of viewing society from the outside. The question of perspective interests him, as illustrated by his looking at a tree from several different windows, "le voyant, selon le cadre dans lequel il s'insérait, grandir, rapetisser, s'élancer, se ramasser, se perdre dans l'ordonnance des peupliers voisins, ou au contraire se développer dans une majestueuse solitude" (218). On his last visit to the country he had been struck by the difference in his enjoyment of the cycles of nature and the view of a young neighbor woman, who had been terrified "par sa monotonie comme un cercle infernal dont on a perdu tout espoir d'échapper" (226). In both cases and in that of his boyhood friends, it is his mobility which makes possible the difference in perspective.

His mobility is apparent throughout the novel; he has no permanent home, living in a rented apartment, in hotels, or in his rented house in the country. He is constantly on the move and has, in addition, another identity, his prewar self. The narrator tells us that Marat is accustomed to separating his life into compartments, "à éviter les interférences entre les divers milieux où il évolue" (402). In Paris he knows by name and is known by the proprietors of many bars and nightclubs whose clientele have nothing to do with the Resistance. When at loose ends he always knows someone he can call. The evening spent at Elvire's apartment in company with collaborators, black-marketeers, and bons vivants is an example of this aspect of his life. At other times he prefers to be alone: "Il aimerait se trouver seul, mettre de l'ordre dans ses souvenirs, dormir enfin" (427). He always has an escape route of one kind or another. On the journey south on the train, he escapes the crowded car by simply walking into first class, where he can escape even the thought of his fellow passengers on the other car, especially the anguish and tenderness of an elderly Jewish couple:

> Il a gardé de l'enfance le pouvoir de diriger ses rêves, il peut à son gré effacer les souvenirs pénibles ou honteux, il ignore les obsessions (sauf à l'époque où il aimait B.) et le remords (sans exception), il peut à volonté s'interdire le soir de penser à l'événement fâcheux qui se produira le lendemain matin, c'est un homme heureux. (208)

This emotional distance is analogous to physical distance and the perspective it permits, illustrated by the bombardment of another section of the city as viewed by Rodrigue and Marat. The narrator compares them to a spectator watching "un choc de nébuleuses" (144):

> S'il n'a pas cédé à la toute première panique que tant de récits entendus sur l'horreur des bombardements tenaient prète en lui il demeure froid et impassible. . . . De si loin, le déroulement inexorable du bombardement n'est pas sans lui procurer un certain plaisir, comme s'il en était l'ordonnateur et s'en trouvait démesurement grandi. (144-45)

Marat recognizes the disadvantages of mobility and the illusion of power gained by distance. He compares himself and the other members of the Resistance to "promeneurs solitaires [qui] . . . continuent à chercher à tâtons leur chemin dans la nuit" (290). He and they really never know the actual results of their work; they know, for example, that they blew up a train, but they do not know whether the German general was on board or not. Marat sees all his work in this way: "Les événements qu'il déclenche rebondissent dans la nuit; quelquefois un écho lui revient" (292). Because of this he gets no sense of progress: "Il n'a jamais l'impression d'aboutir. Tout se passe généralement comme dans ces rêves où l'on monte un escalier, on se dépêche, on s'essouffle, on halète, les jambes s'épuisent à l'escalade, on est toujours sur la même marche" (296). This feeling is a result of the work itself; being a true "promeneur solitaire" involves a different set of problems. Marat has always been a passerby. His retreat in the country has only been rented, and he knows nothing about the people to whom it belongs. In a drawer he finds some letters belonging to that family. The narrator writes:

> Depuis quelques dix-huit ans qu'il vit dans des "meublés," sordides ou fastueux selon les époques, il a souvent découvert des indices qui, par contraste, mettent en évidence sa condition de perpétuel passager; même au coeur des grandes villes, il est toujours cet hôte d'une île en apparence déserte, qui sursaute en découvrant les traces des vrais propriétaires du lieu. (219)

Marat tells Annie that even if he joins the Communist Party he will still be a promeneur solitaire. He uses the example of a person on vacation in the country, where everyone else is continuing about the tasks of daily life, and compares this person to "un personnage facultatif que le peintre a ajouté gratuitement sur le tableau" (289), but who is in danger of receiving a stray bullet. Speaking of the section of Paris which he calls the "creux," he says:

> Il n'est certes pas sans signification que, chaque fois que je suis désemparé, j'aboutisse dans ce quartier comme le navire sans gouvernail qui glisse irrésistiblement vers le Maelstrom. . . . Ainsi, tous ceux dont les liens avec leur milieu, les ancres, les amarres sont rompus . . . échouent finalement au point le plus bas de la capitale. (385-86)

There are many comparisons of the "intellectuel en chômage" and the "homme à la dérive." The danger of being a "promeneur solitaire" is that one drifts aimlessly into the "creux," or is like Pamela's lover who read Nietzsche "de travers" and became a collaborator: ". . . 'intellectuel en chômage,' homme à la dérive: avec un peu de peur dans les tripes ça fait les pires des salauds" (24).

Mathilde is another survivor from Marat's life before the war and is an example of what Marat could have become. She describes him as she knew him before the war: "le plus égoïste des hommes, le plus léger, celui sur lequel on peut le moins compter; un homme de plaisir, un jouisseur" (43). She has given up all freedom of choice and has become the kind of person whose behavior is completely conditioned by "la tuberculose, le jeu ou l'amour-passion" (107). She, like Marat and his boyhood friends, rebelled against the values of her family, who answered by cutting off her funds. She is actually still a child: "Il est . . . plausible que toute femme qui ne possède pas son indépendance économique demeure une enfant" (187). She is a compulsive gambler; even when she has money which she could use for the necessities of life, she keeps it for gambling purposes. She is a drug addict; when she and Marat were lovers she would begin "manufacturing" herself in the morning with alternate doses of cocaine and opium according to "l'image romantique d'elle-même dont elle se faisait un idéal" (62) and would set out in the evening "comme un vaisseau qui s'abandonne au vent après que les armateurs l'aient longuement, amoureusement préparé pour un long voyage" (63). Marat thinks he owes to his "bonne race montagnarde" the fact that he was able to escape "ces plaisirs du monde des fantômes" (63). Mathilde has always lived her life according to her passions, and now Dani, her last hope, is in love with a young girl: "Une femme de mon âge, ça ne désintoxique pas du garçon qu'elle a dans la peau" (54). Keeping Dani has become the one obsession which rules her life.

Another possible response to the danger of being an "homme à la dérive" is that of Frédéric, who, according to Annie, joined the Party for the same reasons people once entered convents, because it offers "une doctrine aussi précise qu'un dogme et exige de ses membres une discipline absolue" (267). Marat and Annie both see this as part of his refusal to face life: "Perinde ac cadaver: le moyen le plus efficace d'échapper à la vie . . . sans jeu de mots" (269). Marat compares Frédéric's kind of "conversion" to conversions to Catholicism in the period between the two world wars, which like drugs, poetry, cruises around the world, and the rebirth of occult sciences were, according to Marat, a means of escaping bourgeois society. This attitude of the "intellectuel en chômage" is contrasted with the militant worker faced with the responsibility of a strike, for whom Communism is in no way a "paradis artificiel" (271). In the eyes of Marat the "true" Communist does not enter the Party because of the discipline, but accepts the discipline for the moment in view of the ultimate aim,"la liberté individuelle la plus totale" (270).

Frédéric's "platonic" love for Annie is another example of his refusal to face life, of his tendency toward abstractions. Marat, recognizing his debt to Stendhal and his theory of "cristallisation," calls this "amour-idée fixe" and does not consider it love because it involves only the head and the heart and not the whole person. In opposition to the loves of Frédéric and of Mathilde, which are seen as means of escaping life and its choices, Marat speaks and writes about what he calls "real" love, which is an organic process:

> Le plus bel amour est celui qui naît, croît, fleurit et meurt, comme une plante, comme un arbre, comme un homme . . . comme le noyer vieillissant de mon village de Bresse avec ses bras enfin figés à la limite d'un voluptueux étirement . . . ou d'une douloureuse crispation. (142-43)

In his prewar journal he laments the increasing separation, "sans doute normale à mon âge," between this kind of love and "la sexualité théâtralement organisée par une maquerelle qui possède bien son métier" (193), but he insists that the two are not mutually exclusive. Each can be experienced separately or both at the same time; an organic whole can be born, grow, flourish, and die within the space of an hour or two just as well as over a long period of years. What is important is the process and the wholeness of the experience of the "corps à corps": "C'est une grande aventure à laquelle participe l'homme tout entier: tête, coeur et ventre. Il n'est rien de soi-même qui n'y soit engagé" (177). It is an important experience because it requires all of the individual and because it allows no cheating:

> Nu à nue dans le silence du lit il n'y a plus de tricherie possible. Le langage ne permet plus d'éluder le réel, le sophiste se trouve au pied du mur; il faut faire ses preuves. La guerre exige la même loyauté. C'est pourquoi l'homme noble n'admettait que deux occupations: la guerre et l'amour. (171)

Theatrical sexuality within the confines of a bordello is perhaps one of the most perfect examples of the combination of the natural and the artificial, of savagery controlled by civilization.

The concept of the controlled organic process is very important to Marat. He is always conscious of the historical moment in which he lives and seems to pride himself on understanding his time in its historical perspective better than most people. He sees the history of mankind as an organic process in which man has now reached "sa crise de croissance, sa crise de conscience, sa maladie" and comments upon the "drôle de sort" which is his to be living "la toute petite portion de la vie de l'homme qui m'est échue juste au moment où il fait sa maladie" (370). But there is no historical fatality: "Il ne faut pas croire que les crises capitalistes engendreront nécessairement l'état socialiste.

Le torrent ne produit de l'électricité que si l'homme l'y contraint" (282-83). Marat is convinced that man can use nature for his own practical and aesthetic purposes. In his retreat in the country he imagines "la végétation folle . . . la forêt vierge" being transformed "en parc à l'anglaise, en verger normand, en jardin de curé" (220). The finished product will represent not only his mastery of nature, but his own tastes and style, his personal mark as proof of his mastery over it. The same principle appears when the narrator writes of silk stockings: "Le bas de soie ajoute à la jambe ce qu'ajoutent au paysage l'allée exactement tracée, le massif taillé, le gazon tondu: il stylise, parachève, parfait" (365). In order to change or dominate nature, man has invented all kinds of instruments or machines, which in turn can threaten to dominate him; but in this novel man can tame them just as he can tame wild beasts. This fact is illustrated by the radio which brings all the voices of the world into the farmhouse of the Favert family; it is "un animal tout à fait domestiqué" which participates in the life of the farm like "une créature vivante, un personnage" (237).

The very concept of revolution is based on the belief that directed change is possible in society, which is made by man. Marat characterizes the "homme de gauche" as the one who believes change is possible and the "homme de droite" as the one who believes it is not possible. Annie doubts the efficacy of revolution and says that man will always exploit man, but Marat counters that this is what the enemy wants her to believe: "*Vanitas vanitatum et omnia vanitas*: la plus efficace des formules de dressage" (277). He, however, says there will always be "hommes de gauche" and "hommes de droite": "Il ne faut ni rire ni blâmer. On retrouverait aisément cet antagonisme à travers toute l'histoire de l'homme. Il est plein de sens" (277). This perspective may make sense, but the problem remains whether the individual is determined by factors over which he has no control or whether he can choose freely to be one or the other.

Consonant with his preference for experiences of the "whole" person, Marat holds that people as individuals or as groups act and react as a result of past experiences, especially those in which they have felt shame or humiliation. Denying that the French people are by nature cowardly, he holds that they did not fight in 1940 because at that time fighting did not correspond to any "besoin profond de leur être," whereas they are eager to fight in 1944 because they have been oppressed and humiliated: "ils ont un affront à venger" (87). His definition of revolution is "la dignité reconquise dans le combat lucide, la dignité des camarades de travail, des camarades d'humiliation" (22). He explains why he could not have become a collaborator:

> pas depuis le jour où j'ai dû dire "bonjour, patron," pas depuis le jour où les porteurs du journal où j'étais rédacteur se sont mis en grève et où il fallut empêcher les "jaunes" de mettre leur voiture personnelle à la disposition du service de vente. (24)

It would appear that the difference between Marat and his boyhood friends can be accounted for, in part, by this feeling of shame in combination with circumstances allowing revenge upon those causing the shame and "reconquest of dignity" in the company of "camarades." However, in an excerpt from Marat's journal we read:

> Qui vit dans des conditions d'esclave a évidemment une mentalité d'esclave. Devenu libre, il pensera en homme libre. La grandeur de la vie, c'est que l'esclave, un jour, se libère, crée lui-même sa condition d'homme libre; c'est aussi inexplicable que la chenille devenant papillon.
> Métamorphoses et révolutions: ainsi procède la vie. (111)

Speaking of employees who occupied their store in 1936, Marat says:

> Ils étaient ahuris de joie. Pas du tout à l'idée des congés payés ou d'une augmentation de salaires. Mais l'acte d'audace inouï qu'ils venaient d'accomplir . . . leur faisait entrevoir pour la première fois que l'ordre des choses qui les

> contraignait à travailler toute la journée, toute la vie, pour un salaire dérisoire, à trembler devant le chef de rayon, etc., n'était pas le seul ordre possible, qu'il leur appartenait de le modifier, qu'eux aussi pouvaient espérer le bonheur. Ils venaient de découvrir la possibilité de bonheur. (283)

This is, of course, a concrete example of the caterpillar, thinking it is trying to become a better caterpillar, suddenly finding through action that it can become a butterfly. Marat uses this same image of natural metamorphosis to compare the members of the Resistance to the generation of the thirties, who lived in a continual not yet, and to a peasant who had been through the Civil War in Spain and who lived in an eternal nevermore. In contrast to them, the members of the Resistance feel hope all around them: "Nous allons changer la face du monde, ouvrir le cocon où frémit déjà l'homme nouveau . . . . Tout peut encore rater, mais la bataille est engagé et son issue dépend de ce que nous serons capable de faire" (158). Thus the war itself is seen as the revenge against the oppressor, making possible the postwar world in which the real metamorphosis of man can take place.

The war can therefore be considered a preparation for just such a metamorphosis, eliminating the parts of the old form which are not needed for the making of the new. Marat is prepared to take part in the building of the new world because of the choices he has made in the past, for which he congratulates himself. This new world will, of course, be different from the other, and he can "sans honte, sans ce sentiment de dérisoire" take his place with his comrades in public life: "Il jouera le jeu, s'engagera, se compromettra. . . . Il pourra 'faire carrière,' devenir, pourquoi pas? un officiel" (163-64). There is never any doubt about life being a game; it is simply a matter of choosing which game one is to play. But in the midst of optimism there is the lingering fear of failure, of playing a losing game. He writes in his journal: "Mais que ferais-je si jamais tout ce que nous sommes en train d'entreprendre vient à rater? Ce soir encore, je suis hanté par la mort de Lorca" (198). He had previously said that he was haunted by a feeling that he had missed his destiny by not fighting and dying in the Spanish Civil War. After all, a man does not really know when it is time to break out of the cocoon; he can be mistaken. Marat has the same fear of failure or of aiming too high when talking with two young militants in the country who have a variety of confused hopes about the victory: "Marat, tout en les écoutant, tremblait pour elles et pour tous ceux et celles qui attendaient trop de la 'victoire'" (227). He continues to be bothered by the thought that the new world will not result from the present conflict and asks Rodrigue what he would do if that happened. Rodrigue answers that he would probably work for the Party educating and organizing the working class, but Marat is not sure Rodrigue understands what that involves: ". . . les meetings, les revendications au jour le jour, la préparation des élections, la bureaucratie du Parti . . . finis les romantiques F.T.P." (166).

Marat recognizes that the truth about an organic process is that it is not reversible. In his discussions with Rodrigue and with Annie he seems to be superior to them because they are viewed as children without his experience or powers of reason. Of Rodrigue, Marat says: "Je suis idiot d'avoir pris un adjoint qui n'a pas l'âge de la raison" (324). Children are incapable of reasoning because they have not yet reached that stage of development. Marat thinks of Annie as a child who has not yet grown up: ". . . elle vit un drame sans le savoir, cela arrive aussi aux enfants, elle ne sait pas ce qu'elle fait, elle agit sans discernement, elle ne sait pas ce qu'elle fait, elle n'a pas l'âge de la raison" (369). Some people, however, remain children all their lives. Rodrigue says of Frédéric's intention to become a professor after the war: "C'est évidemment, par excellence le métier qui permet d'éluder le réel; à parler de Cicéron à des enfants de quatorze ans, on échappe au présent, aux présences." Marat deems this "une manière de demeurer irresponsable, comme un enfant" (172). Marat looks upon his life between the two wars as such a prolongation of childhood and uses childhood play terminology to describe its "caractère provisoire": "'Ça compte pour du beurre,' disent les enfants quand la vraie partie n'est pas encore commencée, quand on joue à l'essai. Tout ce que nous faisions entre les deux guerres 'comptait pour du beurre'" (21-22). He is now ready to take his place as an adult in the adult world, but part of the preparation for the metamorphosis is to ascertain under what conditions this will be possible for him.

Even though he is an adult in many ways in relation to Rodrigue and Annie and can help them to clarify their thinking about life, his relation to the world of work and to money has in the past not been satisfactory. He has experienced working for money, doing work he does not like, and he sees it as a humiliation, in which the "patron" is analogous to the father, the oppressor. Selling one's time for a salary is many times compared to prostitution. Trying to explain to Annie the difference between workers and students, Marat compares the worker to a prostitute: "Le travailleur est généralement contraint, pour 'gagner sa vie,' de se consacrer à une tâche qui ne répond à aucune nécessité intime, à aucune vocation; contraint d'échanger son travail contre un salaire, de vendre à un autre homme son temps, sa vie" (286). Trying to help her understand this feeling, he says: "Pour un homme de coeur c'est une humiliation <u>impardonnable</u>. Sentez-le en femme: le salarié se trouve dans la situation d'une putain, comme elle, il se vend" (286-89). For Marat this situation is changed if the worker becomes a militant, in which case the factory becomes a battlefield on which the worker is equal to the "patron" because he is fighting, thus conserving his dignity. Marat himself is completely happy at this moment because he is doing what he wants to do, what he would do anyway even if he had no need of money. Even though he receives a salary, he does not consider himself "salarié" because there is no separation between his personal budget and his work budget because "la vie du service et ma vie propre . . . ne sont qu'une seule et même vie. Ce n'est qu'ainsi que je puis rester libre à l'égard de l'argent" (304). He sees the money he receives, not as the purchase price for a commodity, but as "un levier, un moyen d'action" (304), allowing him to do his work, which is also the work of those who are paying him. Before the war Marat and Elvire had worked on the same newspaper and had shared the same smile concerning their friends who "faisaient carrière," and she tells him that he will continue the rest of his life to "jouer avec les mots" (334). Marat answers:

> C'est sympathique, c'est de bon goût (comme nous entendons le goût) de jouer avec les mots, preuve de finesse, de sensibilité . . . j'aimais cela comme vous avant la guerre; mais il faut enfin cesser de jouer, sortir de l'enfance, devenir sérieux, c'est à dire, comme moi, se faire une situation sociale. (335)

(It will be twenty years before Vailland, in and through La Truite, fully assumes this social situation by playing with words and at the same time selling himself and proving himself to those who know his value). In 1944 Marat is lucid enough to realize that he does not have the possibilities for the future which Rodrigue and Annie have, simply because of his age and previous experience--the parts of himself which will carry over into any metamorphosis.

One component of his new form as of the present transitional form is his use of reasoning in search of lucidity, which informs, gives form to, the novel. He looks back on his past and analyzes it in order to understand, in part, how he was influenced by his environment and his education and how he differs from his friends. The technique of the novel insures that the reader is aware of what is going on in his mind as he analyzes what he is doing and what others are doing. Seeing Frédéric for the first time and recognizing that his distrust of fat men must be hereditary, he says to himself: "Attention, j'ai une fâcheuse tendance au 'racisme!'" (12). Recognizing the danger, he can be on his guard against it. Reading Xenophon at the end of the novel and reflecting on heroism, he analyzes the characteristics of the men he is joined with in the Resistance to find what they all have in common which makes them heroes. It is his uneasiness at not being able to rationalize Mathilde's behavior which keeps it constantly on his mind so that, when a chance association between Elvire's profile and that of a girl he was infatuated with in his youth reminds him of how he felt then, it is all made clear. He describes this uneasiness to Elvire as a "borrowed" feeling, a state of "disgrâce" like dancing out of step (334-35). When he explains to Rodrigue that Mathilde, thinking Dani had an unimportant job in the Resistance, must have turned him in to the Germans so that he would be grateful to her for releasing him, Rodrigue wants to know how Marat learned this. He answers: "En réfléchissant. . . . Toutes les <u>anomalies</u> que nous avions constatées dans son comportement, s'explique en fonction de mon hypothèse" (360). There are other types of uneasiness which he refuses to submit to rational analysis: "Il se refuse à tenir compte de son malaise, ne voulant pas fonder un jugement sur un sentiment confus, une angoisse, un état défectueux du plexus solaire" (309). In this case he waits for further facts before making a judgment. When he introduces Caracalla to Annie and the eyes of the latter meet, "Marat en éprouva un déplaisir dont il prit conscience" (390). He then proceeds to enumerate the factors which have probably contributed to Annie's elevated opinion of Caracalla.

Throughout the novel he is continually watching himself and analyzing the reasons for his moods and his behavior; he also analyzes the results of possible courses of action and can refuse pleasure in favor of a lesser pleasure which better suits the circumstances, as seen in his line of reasoning leading up to the evening with Elvire and her friends. As Marat says in speaking of his relation to money, what is important for him is equilibrium. To achieve this state he does not use drugs as Mathilde does, but he takes barbiturates when he wants to get a good night's sleep and amphetamines when he needs to be particularly alert, but he knows by experience exactly what the effect will be:

> Il regarde l'heure au cadran lumineux de son bracelet-montre. Il calcule dans combien de temps l'ortédrine agira. Il guette l'effet de la drogue; généralement l'allégement commence par les jambes, puis comme un vent léger qui chasse les brumes matinales, monte en lui, se répand progressivement dans tout le corps, libère enfin les paupières, dissipe le rideau opaque qui pesait sur le front. Il ajourne à ce moment-là la décision à prendre. (274)

The action of the drug leaves him free to direct it: ". . . elle augmente le _tonus_ d'une manière générale mais on peut en aiguiller l'effet, au choix, vers tel ou tel domaine, effort musculaire ou effort intellectuel" (282). When he decides to get drunk, he drinks, but he still maintains a state of "somnambulant lucidity," the state in which he unravels the riddle of Mathilde's behavior. But, just as with his "situation sociale," he has not quite reached maturity yet:

> Il était furieux de s'être laissé aller à boire deux pastis à jeun: effet de l'alcool ou malaise à la suite de la conversation avec Mathilde, toute la légèreté, le printemps intérieur qui avaient enchanté sa matinée avaient fait place à une torpeur maussade. Il demeurait, malgré les approches de la maturité, extrêmement sensible à ces sautes du "temps intérieur" qui avaient fait le tourment de ses jeunes années. (59-60)

Experience and lucidity are two ways to prevent these weather disturbances; playing social games is another. Marat feels that a certain amount of such game playing is necessary for normal relations between human beings, and he thinks that the inability of his wife to play such games was one of the reasons life with her was so difficult. In his prewar journal he finds a passage where he writes of the exhaustion caused by living "réellement" with someone all the time, by not being able to have "des rapports inoffensifs par quoi les humains essaient de se dérober," by having to compromise oneself without cease (190). Marat himself is adept at social games, especially with women, as illustrated by the restaurant scene between him and Annie, in which the reader is made aware of the difference between the words spoken and the thoughts of Marat, of the ease resulting from long practice, and the positive effects of this ease on the girl. Frédéric describes it very well when he thinks that Marat "avait l'habitude des femmes, il connaissait toutes les ficelles du jeu d'amour, c'était un 'vieux libertin,' un 'séducteur'" (400).

Frédéric, who realizes his resemblance with Frédéric Moreau, also looks upon love as a game, but he does not know how to play it and agonizes over the "aisance" and "naturel" of a young couple in a restaurant. Their behavior looks just like that of Marat, but his is the result of long experience and practice. Frédéric neither feels the one nor knows how to proceed in the other. His view of what is happening to Marat and Annie is expressed in terms of trapping an animal, "l'innocente . . . pieds et poings liés, bêtement fascinée" (401). Chance never seems to work for Frédéric, but Marat recognizes its existence: "Il faut toujours laisser une porte ouverte à la chance: j'ouvre la porte, c'est ce que nous pouvons faire, nous en sommes là" (367). His explanation for his not being arrested when Frédéric was is that "la chance m'aime" (422).

Thus Lamballe-Marat in the spring of 1944, having taken stock of himself and having proved himself in dangerous and in amorous circumstances, accepts even Frédéric because "ils ont mené le même combat, ils ont résisté côte à côte, ils sont tous deux de la race qui dit 'non'" (433). Thus armed, he faces the new world. It is obvious that Marat is a "libertin" in the usual acceptance of the word and in the way Vailland defines it. His every effort tends toward being the active subject rather than the passive object. What makes Mathilde's betrayal so unpardonable is that, had he fallen into the trap, he would have been imprisoned, tortured, and perhaps killed; he would have become an object. He remains an amateur in that he likes his work and knows how to do it and is not like the journalists he meets in a bar whose lives were so enmeshed with their professions that they collaborated with the Germans. It is evident that if he does in the future join the Communist Party, it will not be in the way Frédéric joined, but as the result of lucid weighing of his decision. His seeking a "situation sociale" is not something forced upon him by someone else, but is what he feels he owes to himself and to his maturity.

In reality Vailland was not as "disponible" for the future as was Marat. At the time he was writing Drôle de Jeu, he was living with his wife Andrée. His first cure for cocaine addiction in 1942 was followed by a second one in 1947, the same year he divorced Andrée. Les Mauvais Coups, published in 1948, is the story of a man who is trapped in a marriage, who explores how he reached that point and how he can escape, and who succeeds in escaping. The first image in the novel is of a caged owl, by nature a night bird, forced to live in the sunlight. Milan, the protagonist of the novel, is presented as a bird of prey trapped in just such a cage, in this case his childhood and his marriage to Roberte, which are inextricably linked.

The action of the novel takes place during the three weeks preceding the fall equinox in September 1947, but Milan and Roberte relate their lives and the history of their love to Hélène, first together and then separately. The book is divided into nine chapters, like the nine months of a gestation period. The first chapter is devoted to a duck hunt, during the course of which the "rapport de forces" between Milan and Roberte is made clear, and to meetings with neighboring peasants, Radiguet, Radiguette, and Auguste, and with Hélène, the young school mistress. In the second chapter Hélène visits Milan and Roberte that same evening, and they tell her the stories of their lives. The third chapter relates the birth of the calf later that same evening until dawn the next day; it is a difficult birth during which Roberte, who has the right kind of hands, has to reach inside the womb to straighten the calf's legs. The fourth chapter covers the events of the following week including Milan's telling Hélène about the death years earlier of Octave, his friend and Roberte's lover; and the regular Sunday visit of Duval, Hélène's fiancé. The fifth chapter recounts the evening spent at the casino at Aix the following Wednesday, at which time Milan loses half of the money they had set aside for a year in the village, but he does not tell Roberte. The sixth chapter relates the events of the following day, during which Roberte applies make-up to Hélène and tells her the story of Juliette, Milan's most important love since his marriage to Roberte; Milan kills the black bird; and he and Roberte have a fight in which they actually come to blows. The seventh chapter relates the events Friday through Monday afternoon, including the visit of Duval and Hélène, the gathering of the pears by Milan and Hélène, and her declaration of love for him. The eighth chapter is the letter which Milan writes to Hélène that same night, explaining lucidly the "rapport de forces" between him and Roberte. He places it unsealed in a book, hoping Roberte will read it. The ninth chapter relates the death of Roberte on the day of the equinox, Milan's departure from the village, and the beginning of his new life.

Hélène explains to Duval that Milan's sojourn in the village is a kind of retreat in the desert for purposes of self-examination (114). This is obviously what Milan has told her and reflects a rather romanticized image of himself, but he does examine himself much as Marat did in the midst of action, whereas Milan is obviously the "promeneur" on vacation in the country, but he is not "solitaire." The time in the country is presented as the fulfillment of a childhood dream: "Pour la première fois de ma vie, j'ai gagné assez d'argent d'un seul coup pour pouvoir vivre au village tout le cycle des saisons. J'y rêvais depuis l'enfance" (30). Milan's birth at the end of the novel is an escape from the womb into a life where he can develop freely. He remembers once having wondered why one did not eat stillborn calves and being given the answer: "Ce n'est pas de la viande _faite_":

> Le mot lui avait plu. La chair comme l'homme, comme l'amour, comme un livre ou comme le monde de l'homme, doit d'abord _se faire_. "Il est bien vrai," pense-t-il . . . "que le veau qui n'est pas encore détaché de sa mère n'est pas _fait_, pas davantage que la larve dans le cocon. Il ne sera pas _fait_ non plus tant qu'il n'aura pas été sevré; on n'envoie pas de veau à la boucherie avant le sevrage; il faut qu'il _se fasse_ dans sa singularité." (95-96)

The opening imagery is based on the approaching equinox and the fortieth birthday of Milan, on the possibility of metamorphosis, and on Milan's desire not to spend his life sleeping. But he is the victim of a nightmare in which a large black bird is trying to scratch his eyes out; when he has this nightmare he often tries to strangle Roberte. It becomes apparent that the black bird, incarnate in Roberte, represents the myths and fantasies of which he was the victim in his youth. The novel is an effort to look at these myths, to see what in them is true, and to rid himself of what is not true or of what is keeping him from developing as he should. It is equally apparent that Roberte also incarnates a part of himself, his youthful self, which must be destroyed if he is to "agir" rather than be "agi."

One set of myths involves professional choices; Milan now realizes that his youthful outlook was the result of cultural conditioning. When he first met

Roberte, fifteen years prior to the time of the novel, he had "la peur panique de manquer totalement d'argent" (57) and was working at a boring job with a press agency, a job which gave him no satisfaction and left him too exhausted to do anything else. He explains to Hélène that he thought his professional choices were quite limited. He envied manual workers, but was persuaded that their work required some kind of "entraînement natif" (58) which he did not consider himself strong enough to attempt. He did not think he could become an industrialist or a speculator because he lacked a taste for adventure, which "à notre époque, est réservé aux fils de grands bourgeois qui, parce qu'ils ont vu des brasseurs d'argent à la table familiale, ne sont pas persuadés, comme je l'étais, qu'il faille un don spécial pour les grandes affaires" (59). Recognizing cultural conditioning and escaping it are, as with the ideas of romantic love and heroism, two separate actions. Roberte gave him a taste for adventure and taught him what she tries to instill in Radiguette, that one must never believe that anything is too good for oneself. It is the very things which she taught him which now make it imperative for him to leave her.

She also taught him not to be afraid of being without money. During their life together he has held a series of jobs, making enough money to enable them to enjoy themselves for a time, spending that money, and then finding something else. Roberte tells Hélène that Milan is an interior decorator, making clear that he does not do the actual physical work, but that he is the one who has the ideas. She admits that it is perhaps not a "vrai métier," but that he has never had what she would call a real job because he is not "serious." At the casino at Aix they encounter famous people, including a movie star whom Milan had known when he was designing the sets for a movie. In *Drôle de Jeu* Annie had accused Marat of playing at making the others play; here Milan works at providing settings in which others play. The job offer which he receives in the novel and which he keeps secret from Roberte is the supervision of the decoration of a terminal for a steamship company, making more attractive the point of departure and of arrival of ocean voyagers. Although he is no longer afraid of being without money, he still dislikes the necessity of trying to get it; part of his conscious and unconscious motivation for losing the money at the casino is undoubtedly his desire to take the job rather than face a search for employment at the end of the year in the village.

Even in his retreat, he knows what is going on in the world. He knows Duval's chief engineer and keeps up with the progress of the dam at Genissiat, which Duval is helping to construct, and with the problems of Duval's union. When the local peasants discuss a new cooperative, Milan tells them about the success of such cooperatives in Czechoslovakia. But the vacation in the country is judged inopportune by Louvet, the man who offers him the new job: "Aussi bien n'as-tu pas l'âge de la retraite, et le moment de l'Histoire (comme tu dis) n'est pas de ceux qu'on peut légitimement consacrer à la contemplation" (11). Duval is even harsher in his judgment: "Un homme jeune, disons: encore jeune, qui reste oisif quand il y a tant de batailles en cours dans le monde, c'est un déserteur" (120). Radiguette's judgment after the death of Roberte is: "Tous les deux vous n'avez jamais pensé qu'à prendre plaisir. Vous n'étiez pas plus sérieux dans la vie qu'à la chasse. Ça ne pouvait que mal finir" (244). Dreams of childhood must be weighed against present realities.

Another set of myths involves the characteristics of animals and comparisons of animals and human beings. The bird and animal imagery of the first part of the book stresses connections between the names of the species and their natures and makes clear that even in the animal world there are natural champions and those which are not, those which are self-sufficient and those which are not. Characteristics of people are compared to different animals, culminating in the identification of Roberte with the lioness and Milan with the kite (milan in French). Hélène is identified with a young mare and with the dream Milan used to have in which he was chasing a girl whom he desired, a girl who was sometimes a woman and sometimes a mare (94). He says that the "visage de l'amour" appeared like this to him for a long time, with the assumption that it does no longer. According to Milan, Roberte when he first met her was a young hare, a wild animal which cannot be tamed and which dies rather than submit (125). He tells of a young hare which he tried to raise in a cage and which beat its head against the bars, "incapable de transiger avec la loi intime qui lui ordonnait de courir les chaumes et de fuir à perdre haleine, au moindre bruit. C'est ce que j'appelle l'intégrité des bêtes sauvages" (63-64). Domesticated animals are different because their every action is a compromise between their own law and the law of their masters. What impressed him when he first met Roberte was her tremendous strength of character and her integrity: "Elle ne fit pas un geste, ne dit pas un mot où elle ne fût tout entière et rien qu'elle-même. Je n'avais jamais connu d'être moins divisé" (63). He compares himself to a plant, the anti-social nettle: "Comment de la graine d'ortie naîtrait-il autre chose que des orties? La merveille de la nature humaine, c'est qu'à force de lucidité et de patience, un homme-ortie puisse se transformer en chardon . . . ou en froment" (59).

The fact that people are not actually animals or plants is demonstrated by the fact that Milan tamed Roberte because she did not live in the jungle, but in "ma maison," leading to the conclusion that the integrity of wild animals "quand il s'agit d'humains est nécessairement une mystification" (64). This is borne out by the comparison of Roberte and of Octave to the unicorn, a mythological animal created by man's imagination:

> J'aimais et j'admirais Octave . . . non seulement à cause de son talent, mais aussi à cause d'un charme, d'une grâce toute particulière, qui le faisait aussi différent de tout le reste des humains qu'une licorne de toute la race des chèvres. J'étais fier et heureux de connaître un homme fabuleux. (122)

He now sees that his view of Octave was probably "une illusion," while the truth about "integrity" is that it seems to be incompatible with love. In his letter to Hélène he explains that what he loves in her, "la droiture, la santé, l'intégrité," would be destroyed by her love for him if they entered into any kind of relationship. Hélène's admiration for Roberte and submission to having herself "faite" by her illustrate what happens to integrity or purity in a relationship with another person, as does the change in her behavior through association with Milan and Roberte, a change which causes her fiancé to think that she has suddenly become "lunatique."

Roberte at the time they first met was also a duchess: "Seules . . . les duchesses en leurs siècles furent capables d'une telle liberté, mais le temps des duchesses est passé" (63). Roberte spent her early youth with her mother's lover, Uncle, a member of the British diplomatic corps who provided for her material needs and made possible a life of leisure and freedom worthy of a duchess. When Milan met her, she was already an anachronism, so different from everyone else that she seemed to be a unicorn, but unable to catch up with time and to live in accordance with the dictates of the present. Milan admits to Louvet that Roberte gets on his nerves now because of the same qualities which first "enchanted" him: her ease, the fact that she was not "bourgeoise," and the fact that she was "grossière comme une duchesse" (163). Now he is ashamed of her because he thinks the villagers make fun of her and indirectly of him; it is obvious that she has remained as she was, but that he has changed, thus changing his perspective.

The term _duchesse_ has multiple resonances in the novel because of the pears by the same name, which are the only pears which are not wormy this season; but the wind knocks them loose before they are ripe, causing them to fall to the ground bruised and broken. It is apparent that Milan in his youth did not know how to handle Roberte and the idea of freedom in love. The fact that Hélène teaches him what to do with the pears holds out the hope that the younger generation will learn how to handle the problem and that he may be able to learn too, but he learns too late to help Roberte. He refuses to have an affair with Hélène, realizing that the love would destroy what he loves in her just as it did with Roberte. Hélène tells him that the "duchesses" must be picked green and allowed to ripen in the barn. This ripening takes place outside this novel and bears fruit twelve years later in _La Fête_, a novel in which the matter of freedom in love and marriage is examined by a novelist named Duc and his wife Léone.

The principal myth is that of the love of Milan and Roberte, which is related and exhibited to Hélène. During the process she undergoes in relation to them what they went through in relation to each other, but she is a different person from them and has as mentor Milan, who can now see through the myths and interpret them for her, as he does with roulette. Her reaction to Milan and to Roberte mirrors the process of "admiration" and of "cristallisation" which Milan experienced in the early years with Roberte. Hélène tells Milan that she has never known any woman at all like Roberte (109). Milan explains to Hélène the term _flamber_ applied to gamblers,

> avec quel bonheur il exprime à la fois la flamme intérieure qui les dévore, le flux et le reflux du sang entre l'annonce de la mise et le dénouement du coup, les égarements et l'exaltation de leur passion. Le jeu est de la couleur du feu. Roberte est fille du feu. Le jeu, l'alcool ou l'amour ne lui sont que prétexte à flamber. (151-52)

Milan's memories of his early life with Roberte and Hélène's reactions watching Roberte during the birth of the calf and during the evening playing roulette show very clearly that it is Roberte's "flaming" face which Milan loved and which Hélène finds beautiful: "Quand un bûcher est tout entier embrasé, le spectateur, ébloui par l'éclat de la flamme, ne distingue plus la forme des branches ni les noeuds du bois" (151). The brilliance of the flame prevents one from seeing the devouring passion which is causing it. Now Milan prefers a healthier brilliance like the bloom of youth on a young girl's face or a reflected brilliance like that of the full moon (164).

When it is not flaming, Roberte's face has no form of its own; it is "le masque inachevé de l'enfance" (152). She is, like the pears, incomplete, not mature. Like a child she likes to play, to abandon herself completely to the excitement. Playing roulette Milan advises her to change step "pour retrouver la mesure" (146), but reason and measure do not enter into her world. At dawn, after the long ordeal of the birth of the calf, she stamps her foot and says: "Je veux m'amuser" (103). At roulette she plays according to her lucky numbers disregarding the laws of probability. Milan says she does this because she is stubborn: "Elle entend plier la chance à sa volonté. On se comporte à la roulette comme dans la vie. Aucune sorte de prestige n'intimide Roberte et elle se soucie peu des lois" (139). Before the duck hunt, Milan loads their guns, but does not put the safety catch on Roberte's because she gets so excited she forgets to take it off before shooting. During the hunt they do everything wrong, which makes Milan ashamed:

> Il faut savoir ce qu'on fait . . . . Ce n'est pas sérieux. On ne chasse pas avec sa femme, quand on sait qu'elle ne fait rien sérieusement. De vrais chasseurs rigoleraient en nous voyant. J'aime le travail bien fait. Ça me fait honte quand des professionnels se moquent de moi. J'ai honte de la honte que j'aurais si un vrai chasseur nous voyait. Quand

> je fais quelque chose avec toi, je finis toujours par avoir honte de moi. (25-26)

This passage contrasts two different concepts of play, of pleasure, and of life: Roberte's play for pure enjoyment, which is seen as childish, and Milan's more adult, more serious kind of play, which assumes that anything worth doing has rules which must be known in order to play well, to play seriously, and to gain pleasure from it. Those who are really serious about it are "true" hunters, professionals, and these are the judges of how it should be done. There is also a different kind of shame involved. In _Drôle de Jeu_, shame was associated with being an object, with being in a position with no freedom to act. Here it is assumed that everyone is an object in that he is playing to an audience; the problem for the "esprit libre" then remains to choose the audience he wants to play to. The attitudes of Milan and of Roberte toward play are contrasted with the peasants, who do the same thing, but for money to live on rather than for amusement; Radiguette says: "Nos hommes . . . ne savent pas s'amuser" (34). Milan's comment is: "Le plaisir . . . c'est comme un métier. Cela s'apprend, mais peut-être faut-il commencer très jeune" (35).

Milan realizes that knowing how to play the game is of no avail if the "happiness" is missing. At the casino he wins at first because: "Je suis heureux ce soir" (141). It is the same with dancing: "On danse mal quand on regarde ses pieds . . . . Il faut se laisser aller au bonheur" (141-42). This is illustrated a few moments later when he dances with Hélène: "Toute la joie de la jeune fille était partie et elle dansa mal" (145). Milan remembers a humiliation from his youth when he had just finished taking dancing lessons, but was timid with girls. The first girl he danced with left him and sat down saying: "Il faut apprendre à danser" (154). This reminds him of his friend

Octave, who was not timid with girls and who danced beautifully. Octave was a poet at a time when poetry

> s'était raffinée à tel point qu'elle n'était finalement plus accessible qu'à un très petit public, composé lui-même presque exclusivement de poètes. Dans l'extrême jeunesse, un écrivain accepte volontiers la perspective de n'écrire à la rigueur que pour lui-même; il y voit même un gage de pureté. Mais à mesure qu'il mûrit, il ressent de façon plus pressante le besoin d'avoir une audience. (123-24)

Unable or unwilling to change his writing, he found in Roberte "une raison d'être," but committed suicide when she deserted him. Roberte and Octave are both seen as immobile, caught in a way of life which they cannot change or do not want to change.

What Milan once saw in Roberte, and in himself, as freedom and "integrity" is now seen as the "homme-bête" at the mercy of voracious animal appetites. It is this animal which is mated to Milan, who now says that he prizes above everything else "cette possession de soi que Descartes appelle vertu et dont l'autre nom est liberté" (125). From his own experience with Roberte he knows that:

> Ne plus s'appartenir, ne plus se posséder est la pire des humiliations. C'est pourquoi deux amants qui s'aiment de passion ne peuvent que se détester, comme l'ivrogne déteste le vin, le drogué la drogue, le joueur les cartes et le pédéraste les invertis. La passion qui enchaîne l'un à l'autre deux êtres libres ne peut se terminer que par la destruction de l'un ou l'autre; c'est un duel à mort. (127)

In contrast to this kind of bondage, Milan opposes love as a pleasure: "C'est le plaisir de deux êtres qui se caressent et qui se prennent lorsqu'ils se désirent" (224). Speaking of the "fundamental indifference of the choice," he says that all the rest is metaphysics: "le lieu de rencontre d'une foule d'intérêts, de prohibitions, de mystifications et de vilenies" (225). Rather than Roberte's search for passion, he tells Louvet at the end of the novel: "Je n'aime pas le jeu . . . . Les passions sont pour moi <u>d'occasion</u>" (248). Thus passion is accepted for a time when it presents itself, but is not the object of a search and does not imprison the individual.

But after fifteen years, he and Roberte are chained together, not so much by "l'amour-passion" as by all they have been through together, all they know about each other, and all they have done to each other and each one to himself. Before their marriage Milan had to choose between preventing the suicide of Octave and keeping Roberte; his choosing Roberte is completely unjustified if the great love turns out not to be so great. The same thing is true of the humiliations and cowardice of the years together, during which Roberte has permitted him to have casual relationships with other women: "Mais je ne tolérerai pas qu'on me prenne mon mari" (187). She continually goads Milan to sleep with Hélène and get it over with, which to her would be proof that Hélène was of only passing importance. Milan's reaction to the slap administered publicly to Juliette years before and to Roberte's "souillure" of Hélène (plucking her eyebrows, applying garish make-up, changing her hair and her dress) indicates a change in his behavior, if not in his emotions. When he learned of the slap, "Il a crié," but his response to Hélènes's masquerade is "le regard froid" (187). He tells Hélène: "La lâcheté est l'un des aspects de la vie conjugale" (216). Milan places high value on Corneille's "coeur": "Il avait compris depuis longtemps pourquoi Don Diègue demande: 'Rodrigue, as-tu du coeur?'; l'homme sans coeur est celui qui, sous la gifle, ne voit pas rouge, l'homme de bonne race a un coeur de lion" (197). The slap and humiliation administered to Juliette and his not reacting as "homme de coeur" is a proof of cowardice.

But the "homme de vertu" should be able to control the heart, the movements of the blood. Milan is able to describe in detail the process of "seeing red" and feels the progress of the anger through his body (196-97), but after a certain point he is powerless to control it. "Le coeur," which should be proof of nobility and of heroism, has been degraded to domestic squabbles, where it is a sign of weakness, of a lack of "possession de soi," where it is, in fact, proof of Roberte's possession of him: "Me mettre hors de moi, c'est le seul moyen dont tu disposes encore pour m'avoir à toi" (200). Roberte has, in the course of their relationship, given up her pride also: "Je sais ce qu'il en coûte d'être ta femme. Il m'a fallu bien abdiquer tout amour-propre. Pour vivre auprès de toi, il faut apprendre les vertus chrétiennes, l'humilité et la soumission" (195). Their fight in many ways illustrates their years of marriage and furnishes the explanation for the fact that they are still together: "À un moment leurs forces se trouvèrent égales et ils furent contraints à l'immobilité; les yeux dans les yeux, ils se regardaient furieusement" (201). For years they have been held in just such immobility by the equality of the hold each has on the other.

Milan explains their relationship as that of master and slave: "C'était inévitable, l'esclave ne peut que haïr son maître et chacun de nous est esclave par rapport à l'autre, elle parce qu'elle est dans ma dépendance et moi pour m'être laissé ravir ma souveraineté" (224). This interdependence is also expressed by the nurse-patient relationship, in which the nurse needs the patient just as much as the patient needs the nurse, and by the relationship of the mother and the child. Milan has always brought out the maternal instinct in Roberte, as evidenced by her reaction to her first meeting with him and by her behavior toward him throughout the novel: "Ses désespoirs la desarmaient, pourvu qu'ils fussent enfantins" (167). Milan admits to Roberte and to Hélène that he is afraid of Roberte as he was of his mother. She has become the incarnation of all his childhood nightmares of the devouring mother, of all the stifling fecundity of nature and the subterranean passages of the unconscious:

> Elle est . . . impérieuse et tortueuse, éclatante et dangereuse, insatiable comme la reine des abeilles, vorace comme la reine des fourmis; c'est la reine-mère, la grande pondeuse; elle traînerait vingt enfants après elle si elle ne s'était fait faire tant de fausses couches; c'est Junon, Prosperpine et Lucine. . . . elle m'inspire le même effroi qu'à Faust descendu aux Enfers, les Mères. (199)

Roberte has learned how to use the psychological heritage of his childhood as an instrument to keep him bound to her: "C'est la malhonnêteté de Roberte que d'avoir utilisé les noeuds, les replis, les ombres, les sueurs, les paniques, les hontes, tout ce qui d'une enfance opprimée subsiste de louche en un homme, pour entrer en possession de moi" (198). She thus represents for him a whole tradition of trickery, magic spells, and superstition: "_Tu me possèdes_. . . comme un escroc, comme une sorcière et comme un confesseur" (198). The necessity of separating himself from her is emphasized by the death of Octave and by the calf. Roberte delivers the calf from the womb, but the mother survives and the calf dies. The "dialectique du jeu" also makes the separation more imperative. Although in theory each "coup" begins the world, this is not actually true. Any opportunity to escape actually diminishes the probability of a future occurrence of the same thing.

Roberte's dependence on Milan is of a different kind, but is also an outgrowth of her childhood and early adolescence. In addition to the maternal need for the child, she is economically dependent on him as she has always been economically dependent, first on Uncle, then on her mother, preferring this "humiliation" to that of doing work which she did not like. She says she could have discovered radium like Madame Curie: "Mais je n'ai été bonne qu'à aimer Milan et à me faire aimer de lui" (181). She thus feels that it was her nature which caused her to be good for this one thing, and she now considers the bond which unites her to Milan to be "natural": "Elle a appris dès l'enfance que l'inégalité de la femme ne peut être compensée que par les artifices et les illusions de l'amour. Comment lui reprocherais-je de se faire un mérite de m'enchaîner? Elle croit que c'est la loi de nature" (223).

The problem of a mutually satisfactory marriage is illuminated by the discussion between Auguste and Milan. Auguste wants to marry for sexual satisfaction and for companionship, but his life is too hard for the girls in the village, who tend to marry a man who will provide for them materially, a man who will not require them to work, but will let them sleep late: "Il se réjouira . . . en pensant qu'elle est toute chaude sous les draps" (47). This description echoes Uncle's view of Roberte's mother: "She is my convenience" (72-73). Roberte says that he treated her and her mother the same way he treated his dogs, but he later broke into drunken sobbing, saying to Roberte: "Votre mère est une prostituée, mais je ne peux pas me passer d'elle" (71). The village girls are actually prostitutes too, although they use marriage to get the material advantages which Roberte's mother got without marriage. Their husbands end up being trapped as was Uncle, and the girls will be, like Roberte, trapped by economic dependence and advancing age. Or they will be trapped by motherhood or by unpleasant and humiliating ways to avoid it.

Hélène and Duval seem to be different from Milan and Roberte, if only in that they have specific professional goals, which Milan and Roberte did not have at their age. Milan says to Duval: "J'aurais aimé un métier comme le vôtre" (133). When he suggests to Hélène that she will not have to work after marriage and will be able to stay home to care for the home and the children, she is adamant in her refusal of such a life: "Avoir une petite bonne, papoter avec les épouses de ses collègues et mourir à la fin. Ah! non" (214). She says that Duval "accepte volontiers que j'aie dans ma spécialité les mêmes ambitions que lui dans la sienne" (214). However, Duval's violent reaction to her mentioning abortion is an indication of future problems for the young couple, as is their lack of knowledge or experience with any form of birth control. More ominous for the success of their future are his thinking of her as "my" Hélène, his telling her things he does not like for her to do, his lack of understanding when she refuses to make love in the ditches saying that he must respect her, and her maternal feelings while in bed with him.

There is one "good" marriage in the novel, that of Radiguet and Radiguette. Milan explains that sharing the work on the farm has given them an identical outlook on life, the same value system, and that what is usually called love is not so important in their relationship: "Ce qui les unit ressemble davantage à la camaraderie de deux êtres qui participent aux mêmes combats, ou collaborent depuis longtemps au même travail; c'est le lien humain le plus riche, il implique aussi la tendresse et la mutuelle pitié" (226-27). Milan now wonders whether the passion which united him and Roberte for so many years and caused so much grief was really love. He sees it as "une mutuelle mystification" which they accepted because they did not have the courage to be lucid or "cette maîtrise et possession de soi-même qui constitue le seul aspect de la vertu que je sois capable de concevoir et, à l'occasion de pratiquer" (227). Obviously when they first met they were both different people. Now Milan can look back and analyze how it happened, but he could not do that then. Now he sees the future open to "changer la face du monde"; in this new world there is no place and no need for dreams: "C'est dans le visage du réel que nous façonnerons désormais nos rêves" (229). There is also no place for the romanticized idea of absolute love: "Persister à faire du 'Je t'aime' un mot magique qui lie, qui contraint et qui ne doit être prononcé qu'avec précaution, en certains rites, relève de la mentalité primitive, s'apparente au respect du trône et de l'autel" (229-30). The declaration of love between him and Hélène illustrates the new kind of "Je t'aime," a simple statement of fact, not a profession or commitment.

The dream imagery and the heavy-handed mythical and animal imagery of the first part of the book are representative of the fantasy-ridden, impressionable world of his youth, which is seen as a primitive, prerational, surrealistic world of nightmare. This contrasts with Milan's lucid, rational letter to Hélène, in which he explains away all the myths. Roberte, however, cannot be explained away; Milan does use the letter as a weopon to try to rid himself of her. He uses "son adresse et ses artifices" (42) just like Dalila la Rouée in the Arabian Nights, which is the book he is reading during the course of the novel and the book in which he places the letter hoping Roberte's curiosity will cause her to read it. She has, after all, used all kinds of tricks and ruses against him. This manner of killing Robert contrasts with the actual killing of the black bird, effected by shooting at random at the flock of crows which have been noisily accompanying his walk in the meadows. His stalking of the wounded bird through the vineyards and his brutal beating of the bird with the butt of his gun reveal the elemental nature of his hatred, which he overcomes by the actual method of execution which he chooses for Roberte. Not being strong enough to face her and win in "loyal" combat because her tricks would cause him to lose his self-possession, he writes it all down (which is, of course, what Vailland is doing with the novel). He thus attains the synthesis of Descartes and of Corneille which he sees in the characters of Stendhal:

> Ce qui nous fait chérir Julien, Fabrice, Lamiel, Lucien, la Sanseverina, ce n'est pas l'abandon qui soumet à l'amour mais la force de caractère qui permet de l'assouvir, c'est l'appétit de bonheur qui prouve l'homme de coeur et la tête froide qui trouve les moyens de le satisfaire. Les héros de Stendhal ne subissent pas, ils font leur destin. Stendhal est un peintre de la vertu. (228-29)

Roberte, on the other hand, meets the logical end of the wild animal, which is to be hunted down by men; the villagers track her car to the scene of her death in the same way hunters track an animal. Duval's calling Milan a murderer and a coward is seen as the outburt of an inexperienced young man who is not, and has not been, "roué" and who still has ideals of purity. Milan and Dalila la Rouée know that the world is full of dirty tricks and that the only defense against "les mauvais coups" is "les mauvais coups" and/or _Les Mauvais Coups_.

The future envisioned at the end of the novel is the same as that of _Drôle de Jeu_, the repudiation of the "vie à deux" in favor of the virile fraternity: "Je vivrai seul. Je suis trop vieux pour me chercher une compagne comme Radiguette est à Radiguet. Au fait, je ne tiendrai pas tellement à la trouver. Mes camarades seront mes compagnons de travail ou de combat" (230-31). The job offered by Louvet is a specific task which Milan can enjoy; it is the same kind of work he has done in the past, but with a more utilitarian and less frivolous aspect. When asked if he will return to the village, he answers: "Je ne crois pas. Je vais avoir beaucoup de travail" (248). What he would really like to do, as he tells Louvet, is "construire des routes dans le désert, passer six mois à casser des cailloux et dépenser ma solde en deux jours, à me saouler avec des filles" (248). It should be noticed that decorating apartments, movie sets, or stations and building roads are all concrete tasks, which are definitely limited with a beginning and an end. Milan likes to be able to see the whole picture, as indicated by his looking at the landscape with different eyes after losing the money at the casino. He can find no joy in any of it knowing that he will not see the complete cycle of the seasons. But perhaps even this will change, now that he is free to "make himself."

Marat-Milan is now ready to face the world; but while the past was being exorcized, the present has become the future, and Marat's worst fears for that future have been realized. Bon Pied Bon Oeil, written in the first few months of 1950 and published later that year, is a sequel to Drôle de Jeu, relating the lives of Rodrigue and Marat-Lamballe from March 1948 to March 1950. The book has a prologue, two parts separated by the interval of a year, and an epilogue. Third-person narration is relieved by Rodrigue's telling Lamballe about his experiences with Antoinette before their marriage, by Antoinette's telling Rodrigue the story of her life, and by the correspondence between Antoinette and Lamballe. The book recapitulates the outlook of Les Mauvais Coups on the futility of the individual heroic ideal and on love and marriage, but there is added emphasis on the fact that some people are lucky and happy and some are not and on the limits imposed on the present and future by the past.

Rodrigue is evidently intended as an anti-Milan, that is, as a young man who has the lucidity to avoid the mystifications to which the young Milan fell victim, but the character also shows the practical, tactical superiority of a commitment to Communism as opposed to an individual code of morality as a basis for living life in the specific society described in the novel. This society is viewed as being composed of isolated individuals with no cohesive set of values except the egotistical search for survival at whatever costs, a society characterized by hypocrisy, cruelty, and materialism. It is a bipolar world full of jails, prisons, and police, a world where people are either "punis ou punisseurs" (151).

The characters are such obvious caricatures it is difficult to take any of them seriously. Marat is once more François Lamballe, who, after being wounded as a war correspondent and making money in the illegal currency traffic, is now a gentleman farmer raising cattle on the plateau of Aubrac.

Rodrigue, after a period of glory as a soldier and as an attaché to a Communist cabinet minister in 1946, is at the time of the novel a minor functionary, "rentré dans le rang," who accepts social invitations from his director, who is M.R.P.: "Il ne faut pas être sectaire" (34). He lives with his mother and divides his time between his job and his cell and union activities. A chance sexual encounter with Antoinette Larivière results in the birth of a child, which he does not know about until he reads in the paper that she has abandoned the child and has been arrested. He marries her, planning to divorce her as soon as the case is cleared up, but Lamballe and a lawyer convince him to live with her for a while. They settle into a very comfortable domestic life, which lasts until Rodrigue is arrested on what are seen as trumped-up charges intended to embarrass the Communists. As soon as he is arrested, Antoinette contacts Lamballe, who contacts people he knows in the world of journalism, who publish the facts. The police, realizing that only Antoinette knew these facts, take her in for questioning. She refuses to tell whom she contacted, but during the course of the interrogation, she is slapped repeatedly, resulting in the loss of one eye. She continues her efforts to free Rodrigue, while he enjoys himself in prison studying the history of the Convention and falling in love with his young Communist lawyer, Jeanne Gris. When Antoinette finally finds herself, because of her ill-advised machinations, in the position of being blackmailed by one of Rodrigue's guards, she appeals to Lamballe. He comes to the rescue by applying pressure on an official whose past Lamballe knows. Rodrigue is released, and he and Jeanne Gris go off to build the new world while a lamed and castrated Lamballe and a one-eyed Antoinette vegetate in splendor on Lamballe's property, a former monastery of the Knights Templar built on a plateau of cooled lava. They will, however, raise the son of Rodrigue and Antoinette, whose name is Roger.

Lamballe's becoming a war correspondent after the Liberation is seen by the author as characteristic of Lamballe's manner because he had complete freedom of movement and "joua à la guerre, sans en connaître les servitudes, et en subit les risques, sans en connaître les gloires" (10). He is seen as a dandy in the Byronic mold whose illegal activities and search for personal freedom, "ce trafic auquel je dois ma liberté, je veux dire de n'être contraint de me mettre au service de personne pour gagner ma vie," now prevent him from joining the Communist Party, which might be compromised by his presence (11). His need for amusement is seen as a function of a lack of maturity: "Mais tu ne mûris pas. Tu es un vieux jeune homme" (27). His statement: "Je ne suis peut-être bon qu'à faire un soldat" (28) brings to the reader's mind Roberte's opinion of her destiny. His business of raising and cross-breeding cattle is viewed as useful but marginal work, which is aimed at making money and which stresses racial rather than environmental, elitist rather than fraternal values. He tells Antoinette that he still agrees with the Communists, but that he has enough money to remain "provisoirement _en marge_ du conflit" and that he does not care enough for other men or his own reputation to feel obliged to give up his pleasures (190).

He tells Antoinette that he received his wound because he wanted to "tenter l'aventure" (249); the description of the incident in which he, an observer, was wounded contrasts with Rodrigue's experience fighting with the army of de Lattre. Rodrigue was involved in a Jeep accident in which the others were killed or disfigured while Rodrigue received a few minor scratches (226). Lamballe describes himself and Antoinette as "les solitaires qui se promènent au milieu des batailles qui ne les concernent pas" and who "attirent les balles perdues" (249-50). To Antoinette's assertion that nothing concerns them, he answers: "Je crois même que les ôtages que l'on fusille, pour des actes qui ne les concernent pas et qu'ils n'ont pas voulu ou pas osé commettre, sont également coupables à l'égard de l'un et l'autre camp" (250). In the end of the novel, it turns out that his wound was more serious than a simple leg wound, that he was, in fact, castrated, rendering even more ironic his pride in raising prize bulls and his distrust of timid party sympathizers: "Un taureau trouillard n'acquiert jamais de couilles" (23). His castration is made manifest by his boredom at the wheel of his car (176). His tactical position is represented in his advice to Antoinette: "Il faut attendre et voir venir . . . c'est dans la patience et l'inaction que réside souvent l'héroïsme" (182). However, his age and experience have enabled him to understand the intricacies of public life and how to get things done by applying pressure in the proper places. He thus possesses an "excès de puissance": he knows how to play the game, but he does not choose to play it. His actions in the novel are all aimed at helping his friends; it is he who advises Rodrigue and Antoinette to see a lawyer about their marriage, who recommends a lawyer, and who succeeds in obtaining Rodrigue's release from prison, thus disarming himself by using power he had been saving.

Antoinette, daughter of a high school principal who fought at Verdun in 1917, collaborated with the Germans in World War II, and managed to remain free after the war, is presented as a young girl with a penchant for rebellion against parental authority and values and a taste for adventure and romance. She considers herself a member of an unlucky generation, destined to know only financial worries and the stories of their elders who fought in the war. Her estimation of her generation is belied by the fact that her best friend did take part in the Resistance, but did not tell her of her activities until after the Liberation. Rodrigue approves her friend's reticence: "Tu n'avais pas de convictions. Tu aurais désiré aussi passionnément servir les nazis, si c'étaient eux qui avaient comploté dans l'ombre et joué les Robin Hood dans les forêts. Tu n'étais pas sûre" (81). She is the incarnation of the "déclassé," of the "homme à la dérive" of Drôle de Jeu. She is seen to be like most girls her age in this "société en décomposition," as Lamballe calls it (47). In contrast to Lamballe's memories of the days before the first world war when girls showed their social class by their dress, make-up and hair styles, girls now dress alike and use the same kind of make-up, decorate their room in the same way, and listen to the same records, "mais chacune a ses totems et ses tabous personnels" (46). Having no class or group with a value system they can identify with, they go their separate ways, with no real guidance from the older generation. Antoinette thus describes her life before marriage and the early part of her marriage: "Tout . . . me paraissait avoir exactement la même valeur, ou plutôt la même absence de valeur" (191). These people with no class or value system of their own are compared by Rodrigue to weasels. He speaks ironically of the heroic battle between a weasel and a sparrow-hawk and concludes: "Au milieu des guerres et des révolutions, la plupart des bourgeois et des petits bourgeois français continuent de mener, sans ouvrir les yeux ni les oreilles, leur petite vie de belette. Ils ne voient venir ni l'obus, ni la bombe atomique" (84).

In Antoinette's case, the negative revolt against bourgeois values leads to literarily-based dandyism; to a search for adventure in casual sexual encounters, resulting in abortions and a consciousness of the derisory nature of her existence; and to a job taken with no "vocation," but which provides materially for her and her child. She describes her work and her attitude toward it in terms similar to those used by Milan. In contrast to her and to the other girls in the laboratory, there is one girl who is a union delegate and militant Communist, but Antoinette is unable to understand how this girl has the energy to do everything she does. Antoinette's lack of convictions and susceptibility to the kindness which she did not find at home are illustrated by the fact that she was treated so kindly at the Maternity Hospital "qu'elle n'osa pas exiger qu'on remît l'enfant à l'Assistance publique, comme elle en avait d'abord pris la résolution" (86). When Rodrigue asks her why she abandoned the child, she answers: "Ah! . . . je crois que c'est encore mon goût de l'héroïsme" (87). She later explains to Lamballe that her action was "un enfantillage" of which she is not ashamed because it was a gesture against the morality of people like her parents, which she sees as no morality at all, but simply as weakness: "Je n'en dois montrer que davantage de fermeté et de force de caractère; sinon, rien ne me distinguerait d'eux" (178).

But strength and character alone without lucidity and a broad perspective are useless; she did not envision any of the consequences of abandoning her child and was in no way prepared for any of the humiliations heaped upon her during her incarceration. Following these experiences, she finds in marriage a refuge and "la paix de l'âme," because of the strict routine, like that of a convent (191). Unlike Frédéric in _Drôle de Jeu_ who sought such discipline in lieu of facing life because of a fear of life, Antoinette finds in discipline a refuge after having entered life unarmed for the battle. Lamballe later compares her to Rodrigue, saying that Rodrigue's "formation de résistant et de militant l'a mieux armé que vous pour ce genre de combat" (179).

The pattern of her life can be seen in her behavior on the occasion of Rodrigue's arrest. At the time she is engrossed in reading _Mademoiselle de Maupin_ and dreams of it as she vacuums. Her subsequent "heroic" actions are obviously partly conditioned by her reading, but they are not called for in the present situation: it would have been the normal thing to call Lamballe and there was no need not to tell that she had called him. Through their informers the police find out all they want to know and much more than she could possibly know. The fact is that she is utterly alone against the police during her interrogation and is even afraid to call Lamballe because of a fear of phone taps and a lack of understanding of the situation. She realizes that most of the questions of the police are aimed at humiliating her and that "la dignité du politique" is forbidden to her (120). Her isolation is emphasized by the office where she waits between interrogations, which is separated from the corridor by a "baie vitrée" through which she can see all kinds of people with whom she cannot, and does not want to, communicate. She compares the hell of Courteline to that of Kafka, which is not "vulgaire," and decides that the hell of Courteline is exactly what she deserves and she is humiliated by it. She explains to Lamballe that it was not out of loyalty to him that she kept silent but because of her own sense of dignity, her perception of what she owed to herself in the presence of the vulgar ignobility of the police. Lamballe in answer writes to her that he is certain of her courage, but that he is afraid of her integrity and her honor: "C'est la fierté des bêtes sauvages qui les livre sans défense aux hommes" (179). He invites her to come stay with him "à l'abri des ignobles."

Lamballe and Antoinette are obviously intended to be "fils de roi" in the sense Gobineau uses the term in Les Pléïades, superior people who have been pushed into the abyss by the crowd of lesser beings; they make their way back up to the surface but remain "borgnes de l'oeil droit" because it takes a long time to clean away the filth gathered in contact with the barbarism and savagery of the depths (Gobineau 31). However, Lamballe is labelled throughout the novel as an adventurer, and Antoinette says: "Moi, je préfère toujours la liberté, même pour une heure, une minute, une seconde" (218). In their exiled splendor, they spend their time "distracting" themselves, Antoinette by knitting and Lamballe by telling stories of his past amorous exploits and trying to catch the old trout which so far has eluded capture. The question for them, and for the reader, is Rodrigue's question to Antoinette: "Je me demande ce que tu es capable de faire de ta liberté" (218). Lamballe, in a letter to Antoinette, expresses their position:

> Je sais que pour le combattant, le combat n'est pas absurde et que pour les meilleurs des hommes, enfin pour ceux parmi lesquels j'aime choisir mes amis, la vie est un combat, qui signifie quelque chose. Mais ce soir, je ne combats pas. Du haut de ma montagne . . . je suis spectateur et j'ai le coeur navré que la vie m'apparaisse comme "une histoire racontée par un fou, pleine de bruit et de fureur et ne signifiant rien." (199-200)

It is evident that the historical Lamballe for whom this character is named is not the same Lamballe of Drôle de Jeu. Prince Lamballe died forty years before the Revolution, and the use of the name in Drôle de Jeu implied a dead past as opposed to the present Revolution of Marat. In Bon Pied Bon Oeil it is obvious that Lamballe is the Princess Lamballe, confidante of Marie Antoinette, that the Revolution is in the future, but in the near future, and that neither of them will survive the Revolution. They are products of the civilization which must be destroyed, an integral part of which is their conception of adventure, heroism, and freedom.

There is one authentic hero in the novel, although he appears only briefly. Albéran, who has a "beau regard, droit, ferme et pourtant presque tendre" (60), is a former metal worker at Hispano-Suiza who has been a member of the Party since 1925, who fought in the international brigades in the Spanish Civil War, and who has spent ninety-one months in prison, where he completed his political education. At the time of the novel he has remained in "la carrière militaire" and is in the War Ministry. Rodrigue describes him: "C'est le combattant communiste, le bolchevik, un type d'homme absolument nouveau. On n'a pas encore fait son portrait, les écrivains sont toujours en retard sur l'histoire de leur temps; ce sera le héros, le chevalier errant, le Roland et le Roger de l'épopée communiste" (60). He, like Lamballe, received a wound in the thigh, but his was during the war in Spain, and he has accomplished a great deal for the cause since then. It is Albéran who advises Rodrigue to use his own judgment about marrying Antoinette because the Party will survive whether there is a scandal or not. He admires Antoinette's behavior with the police, and she, during her marriage to Rodrigue, always feels more at ease with Albéran than with Lamballe. Arrested at the same time as Rodrigue, Albéran succeeds in making immediate contact with his comrades on the outside, and he, from prison, takes charge of the press campaign and the organization of the protest meeting. However, Lamballe insists that even Albéran could not have been a hero without the right circumstances. He tells Antoinette that she is "orgueilleuse et têtue" and that these are the characteristics of heroes, but she has not had the right set of circumstances.

The character Rodrigue is an experiment, an attempt to see what it would take for someone with a bourgeois or petit-bourgeois background to live in society in order to have some effect on it, to see how a person can be "fils de roi" and not be sullied by contact with society. In contrast to Antoinette and Lamballe, Rodrigue, who was already a Communist in Drôle de Jeu, has no time for pleasure. He no longer goes to the gym, he does not dance well because he is out of practice, and he does not swim well because he never has the time to learn. He accepts tasks like delivering the Sunday Communist newspapers because he is convinced that the task is worthwhile, that even those who buy the papers and are timid and ashamed about it will "understand" one day. Lamballe, however, maintains that understanding will not give them "du caractère" (23). Rodrigue has human contacts, which Antoinette and Lamballe do not have; he knows the habits of everyone on his route and sympathizes with their problems. For him, as for the young militant in Antoinette's lab, the drudgery of the present task is redeemed in the light of the ultimate aim:

> C'est une tâche concrète, un boulot, cela ressemble au travail du mineur, du métallo, du soldat, . . . c'est souvent ennuyeux, comme l'usine ou comme le champ de bataille, cela fait partie de la vie de tous les jours, comme la guerre pour le soldat . . . ou pour un vrai écrivain sa grande oeuvre. (30)

He is, however, not perfect. He had difficulty explaining to his director that a person can take pleasure in making war and still be a pacifist (38), and he has no excuse for having brought home the document which causes his arrest. He is not sure that he is a good militant. Although Antoinette calls him "l'intègre Rodrigue" (159), he does not feel that he is. She uses the term to mean unspoiled and undefiled, while he is concerned with what he sees as the undivided unity of self of the good militant, but he does not agonize over his shortcomings.

As Antoinette and Lamballe both agree, he is still a child, one who has a future and one who can learn from his experiences. One of his strengths is that he sees himself this way too and is not prey to false shame for not doing things he cannot be expected to know how to do. He is not fooled by an idealistic image of himself. He has just finished reading La Chartreuse de Parme when he has to make the decision whether to marry Antoinette. He begins by wondering what Fabrice would have done, but he quickly realizes that he is not Fabrice, Antoinette is not Marietta or Clélia, and the entire structure of society is different; so the novel cannot help him to reach his decision. He, unlike Antoinette, has friends whom he can approach for advice, friends who have the same aims in life as he and whose opinions he respects. In prison he can take as his model heroes of "l'épopée communiste" rather than Fabrice, which, however, does not prevent him from being slightly jealous when he hears all that Albéran has been able to do in prison. This momentary feeling is banished by his realization that he has not had Albéran's experience, that this is his first time in prison. He refuses to dramatize himself and the situation: beginning to feel "banni du genre humain, excommunié," he murmurs: "Pas de Kafka, pas de Kafka," and the feeling soon passes (148).

He is constantly conscious of his responsibility as a Communist; he knows that his private life must be above reproach because: "Je suis communiste, et tout communiste est en quelque sorte un homme public, qu'on ne doit pouvoir salir en aucune manière" (58). He accepts this responsibility and receives in return the rewards of fraternal camaraderie. In prison he is conscious of the fact that his comrades on the outside are looking after his interests; his only concern is how to make the most of his experience. Unlike Antoinette, he was prepared for the police interrogation and for prison: "Tout militant sait qu'il devra un jour ou l'autre livrer ce combat-là, où l'homme est seul contre les forces de la répression, et que l'occasion s'en présentera à l'improviste" (102), and he had long planned how he would act. In jail Antoinette had felt humiliated, furious, and naked when standing before a group of seated men who were questioning her (71). Rodrigue, actually stripped and searched in his most private parts, at first has visions of revenge and even of escape; but after reading a copy of l'Humanité lent to him by a humane guard, talking with his lawyer, and getting a shave, he decides that it was not such a terrible humiliation after all: "Effet à retardement . . . des insomnies imposées deux jours plus tôt par les policiers; c'est la fatigue qui engendre l'angoisse et la honte" (161). What could have been a great humiliation becomes merely an inconvenience to be endured for the good of the cause, just as the prostitutes in jail with Antoinette submitted to anything their customers asked because they were making money to spend on their children. Just as Antoinette had begun to find peace of soul in the routine of marriage, Rodrigue finds in prison the time to do whatever he wants do to, within limits. In contrast to Antoinette and to Frédéric, his retreat is a temporary refuge in the midst of battle, during which he hopes to make himself better able to wage the battle after his release.

Social conventions viewed as sacrosanct constitute a permanent prison for some people. Mother love is denied by Antoinette and by the novel; it is seen as "l'attachement du créancier pour le débiteur, d'autant plus grand qu'il a prêté ou donné davantage" (79) and as not necessarily natural: "La plupart des poissons sont friands de leurs alevins" (75). The prime example in the novel of a social convention raised to the status of the sacred by a primitive people is the "bonds of matrimony," the power of which is illustrated by the marriage of Antoinette and Rodrigue. It is made clear that this marriage, entered into simply to free Antoinette from jail, could easily have trapped both of them for life.

Antoinette begins by being grateful to Rodrigue. Then several incidents cause her to see him in a different light, to see him as someone who loves humanity, who is good probably because he has always been happy, and who glories in his happiness. Having put him on a pedastal, she begins to see new meaning in the household tasks and tries to please him. Then she cares for him when he is sick: "Rien n'est si désarmé sur la terre, qu'entre deux draps blancs, moites du bain de sueur, le corps nu d'un homme malade" (194). They actually have nothing in common; he spends supposed leisure time doing work for the cell and the union. On Sundays they receive friends, who all discuss matters which Antoinette does not understand, while she serves them and does household tasks. But he has now become her husband and she his wife, whom Lamballe calls "la bonne épouse, toutes griffes et crocs dehors pour défendre son homme" (185). She uses two images to explain to Lamballe how she looks on her marriage; in one of them she and Rodrigue press close together in the midst of universal war and chaos "comme si l'emmêlement de nos corps était notre seul et vain secours contre la fureur universelle" (194); in the other, Antoinette, who like Marat reads Xenophon, sees the two of them as the only members of the Ten Thousand who know that they will all die before they reach the sea, but they fight separately each day and spend the night pressed close together: "Et ainsi de suite, jusqu'au jour de notre mort" (195). This is quite poetic and sublime, but it has no relation to the flesh-and-blood reality which is Rodrigue. Her subsequent self-sacrificing efforts to free Rodrigue despite his explicit instructions to the contrary do succeed in freeing him when it is obvious the Party has decided to sacrifice him, but he does not appreciate the value of her efforts.

While in prison Rodrigue, for the first time, tries to clarify in his own mind the kind of relationship he has with Antoinette and decides that he has a wife and child in the same way a tree has leaves: "L'arbre ne se pose pas de questions au sujet de ses feuilles" (171). This is the kind of feeling Lamballe had warned him about when he described marriage as "a sacred institution protected by all the taboos of the tribe." He explained:

> C'est que le lien du marriage est si mystérieusement et si inextricablement noué, que les plus lucides finissent par croire qu'il est _de nature_, et que le couple, comme le plomb, l'or ou le soufre, est _un corps simple_, que la volonté ni la science de l'homme ne peuvent dissocier. (63)

But since Rodrigue is "heureux," he finds "real" love with Jeanne and can then see his marriage to Antoinette for what it was: "Ils ont vécu ensemble, parce que cela se trouvait ainsi, maintenant, il en est autrement" (227).

The love of Rodrigue and of Jeanne is seen as the beginning of the kind of relationship enjoyed by Radiguet and Radiguette. Jeanne's father was a militant metal worker, her grandfather was a socialist who voted for the scission at the Congress of Tours, her great-grandfather was a Communard, and she has known Albéran since she was a child. Rodrigue calls her family "l'aristocratie ouvrière" and calls her jokingly a duchess. The two of them are at first interested in each other only professionally; Rodrigue even tells his guard that she is not his type. But her face begins to appear in his daydreams, and he begins to tell her everything he does and thinks, saying that he has no "domaine réservé," and that she is his "journal intime" (171). They both agree that neither of them has a "jardin secret . . . produit de luxe, réservé aux oisifs, un privilège de classe" (172). It is made perfectly clear that their love is not "l'amour-passion-l'amour idée fixe," but the love which grows like a tree, developing into their mutual declaration of love in the knowledge that the future is theirs: "Jeanne Gris et moi, nous avons des idées claires, des vues justes sur le monde, de la chance, je suis sûr qu'elle danse en rythme, nous sommes heureux en amour" (227).

It is obvious that the novel is arranged so that Rodrigue will not feel any guilt, humiliation, or "mauvaise conscience," which would make him vulnerable in a society of "flics" or which would make him like the young Marat-Milan. Lamballe says to him: "Tu n'as pas une nature d'anxieux" (62). Lamballe says he is innocent; Antoinette says he is good because he has never been humiliated, even by experiences which would have humiliated others; Jeanne says he is Hippolyte, without Phèdre, of course. Rather than being trapped in a boring job accompanied by the "clin d'oeil complice" of his director (217) or in a guilt-ridden marriage faced with Antoinette's staring eye, he resigns his job and goes off to Toulon to work in the office of the dock workers' federation, where he finds excitement, where Jeanne comes frequently to defend workers, and where he finds a sense of fraternity with the workers and their families. He does not even have to face the chore of getting rid of Antoinette, who leaves of her own accord: "Je suis très fatiguée de toi, de ta santé, de ton entrain, de tes entousiasmes et de tes camarades. J'ai mille ans de plus que toi (et le visage mutilé, comme un véteran). Je ne peux pas continuer de vivre avec mon arrière-petit-neveu" (238). This is also the opinion of the reader; Rodrigue is simply not human. Thus within the novel neither Rodrigue, nor Antoinette, nor Lamballe has a tenable "situation sociale" which Marat-Milan hoped to build for himself.

However, within the novel, there is a clarification of the amateur-professional dichotomy, and the novel itself is a statement of position of the writer in relation to an audience. The power of the press is used as a metaphor for the public eye which conditions the action of the individual in a world where there are no secrets. It is through the sensationalized account of Antoinette's abandonment of the baby that Rodrigue finds out about her plight, and it is his fear of such an account identitying him as the father and as a Communist which causes him so much soul searching when trying to decide whether to marry her or not. It is the press stories about Rodrigue's arrest which lead the police to interrogate Antoinette. It is her fear of having Rodrigue soiled by being linked to her in the newspapers which causes her not to press charges against the police. As Lamballe says: "Il n'existe rien aujourd'hui qui ne soit publié quelque part" (11).

There is a positive aspect to the power of the press as seen in the educational possibilities of the Communist press vaunted by Rodrigue and in the fact that Lamballe's publicizing of the arrest of Albéran and of Rodrigue embarrasses the government and brings the matter into the open. For Rodrigue and Jeanne the press emphasizes their involvement in the history of their time: "C'est extraordinaire à quel point leur destin personnel dépend des nouvelles qu'ils lisent chaque matin dans les journaux, cela les fit rire!" (224-25). The fact that Lamballe and Antoinette do not read the newspapers underscores their separation from the world.

Since everything is published and there are no secrets, the important thing thus becomes interpreting what is published, which explains the importance given to Jeanne's youth, during which she listened to Albéran and her father commenting critically on politics and the events of the day as they read the newspapers. In this context "professionalism" is seen as a conscious or unconscious attempt to victimize others by making the simple and accessible seem difficult, inaccessible, and thus secret. Rodrigue's malevolent guard, who occasions the search of his cell and of his person, repeatedly says: "Vingt ans de métier. Jamais une faute professionnelle" (146). He lives by the rules with no attempt at any kind of human contact and is insulted when Rodrigue asks him whether he enjoys fishing: "Je ne suis pas encore à la retraite. Je sais qu'il y en a à qui cela ferait plaisir. Mais je reste solide au poste" (145-46). He uses vocabulary with special meanings obvious only to those who have been in prison or who have worked there: "'Mais vous êtes au secret,' dit-il, sur le ton même dont il aurait pu dire: 'Mais vous ne voyez donc pas qu'il pleut'" (141). Rodrigue remarks on the "amour-propre en quelque sorte professionnel qui incite les S.R. à proclamer que tout ce qui sort de leurs bureaux est EXTRÊMEMENT SECRET" (105-106). In this context the investigating policeman informs Rodrigue: "Il ne vous appartient d'ailleurs pas de décider du caractère plus ou moins confidentiel d'un document que les spécialistes de nos service spéciaux estiment EXTRÊMEMENT SECRET" (105). This is a special case, but the tendency to professional elitism is obvious; only the professionals are really competent to judge matters within their domain and they guard this domain with care.

In contrast with this professional elitism, Rodrigue is conscious of being "un politique," which is compared to service tradesmen, "un plombier avec sa sacoche d'outils en bandoulière, des électriciens avec leur écheveau de fils" (148), each identifiable by the tools of his trade. Thus politics is seen as a trade or skill, requiring a certain apprenticeship; the identifiable tool is "la dignité du politique," which is manisfested "dans son maintien, dans son regard" (148). Jeanne points out: "Les problèmes politiques . . . c'est beaucoup plus simple que les salauds n'essaient de le faire croire" (164). As Milan would have said, politics, like business, requires no native training or special gift; it is like any other skill and can be learned by anyone, provided he start early enough with experienced teachers.

Thus journalism, which in Drôle de Jeu and Les Mauvais Coups was viewed with disdain, is not in itself bad. What is bad is a certain use of journalism, distorting or ignoring facts and trying to mislead. It is seeing journalism as important in itself rather than in its relation to the world. The same holds true for literature in general; Antoinette's actions after reading Mademoiselle de Maupin reveal the dangers of escapist literature and the apparent impossibility of "l'art pour l'art." The seemingly human need for models and the search for them where none was intended suggest that perhaps literature can furnish the models to help change society. In addition, telling "the truth" has a power all its own; when Rodrigue is embarrassed because of having said in the presence of his director that war was the most amusing thing in the world, Lamballe insists that he is the one who used to say that during the Resistance: "Tu as certainement pris plaisir à faire la guerre, mais si tu ne me l'avais entendu dire et répéter, tu n'aurais pas eu le courage de l'avouer, même à toi-même et dans le plus grand secret" (37). So perhaps if a writer keeps writing the same thing, the truth as he sees it, it may eventually be accepted as a fact.

However, Marat-Lamballe-Milan is not yet ready to accept this position. Milan actually cheated when he accepted the repressed childhood as a fact and killed it without looking at it or trying to understand it. The "esprit libre" must not use dirty tricks against itself. There also remains the problem discussed by Lamballe and Rodrigue of seemingly cowardly men who act courageously; if Lamballe had not been castrated, what would it take to bring him down from his mountain? These are the problems faced in Un Jeune Homme Seul, published in 1951. It is the only one of Vailland's nine novels which relates the early life of a character as the events happen, rather than having an adult look back on his youth and tell it to others. It is also the only one in which the time of the novel does not come up to the present in which the novel was written. It is the story of a man imprisoned by his childhood environment who finally proves his manhood; of a petit-bourgeois isolated from the working class, but wishing to be part of it, who is finally integrated with that class in a common struggle. The mythic structure of the novel is obvious; Vailland himself wrote in a letter to Pierre Berger that the first part of the novel depicted "la lutte de Saint Georges et du Dragon" and that the second part was "l'histoire de la Belle et la Bête" (Écrits Intimes 443). The novel also once again makes use of Gobineau, clarifying the concept of the "fils de roi" and identifying the "Pléïades." The novel thus reaffirms the value of some childhood myths, especially that of the existence of unicorns.

Part I introduces Eugène-Marie Favart in Rheims in 1923, when he is nearly sixteen; the events of one afternoon in May and memories occasioned by these events depict his sheltered childhood and his limited view of the world, but also his aspirations toward lucidity and courage. The two-day celebration in Paris of the wedding of his uncle to a girl of the working class broadens his perspective on the world, his family, and himself and adds to his store of experiences. Among the people he meets are a Spanish girl, Domenica, and a Communist worker, Pierre Madru. He faces several tests of his manhood, some of which he passes and some of which he fails miserably, and he returns home. Part II is constructed around the investigation by a Vichy inspector of the death of Madru in April 1943 at the railroad yard of which Eugène-Marie, now married to Domenica, is chief. As in the first part, the actual events cover a period of three days, but the investigation reveals what happened to the characters in the intervening years and precipitates Eugène-Marie's adhesion to the group of those who are fighting for freedom against the forces of repression.

As an adolescent Eugène-Marie, like Milan, suffers from "la solitude bourgeoise"; he lives in a private home situated between two houses in ruins facing the avenue along which pass the working girls from the brick factory. From behind the curtains of the "baie vitrée" of his house he watches the girls walking along the middle of the street laughing and talking together in what he calls their "marche triomphale, précédée d'un solennel sifflement de sirène," which has become his image of "la fierté humaine" (71). He does not really see the girls as they are and does not realize that the pretty shawls which he admires so much are worn in even the bitterest cold. It is not until the wedding that he finds out that they cannot afford coats. Watching them he engages in romantic adolescent fantasies about encounters with these girls, even though he realizes that he would not know what to do and that they would laugh at him because he still wears short pants and has no money of his own. At home he has been over-protected and coddled by a mother who wants to keep him from growing up so he will remain dependent on her, who wants to preserve the "pureté de son coeur" (42).

Like Rodrigue's mother in Bon Pied Bon Oeil, Victoria Favart is a devout Catholic and spends her time in pious parish projects, but she does not have the strength of character which Antoinette saw in Madame Rodrigue. She continually nags her son, as she has obviously nagged her husband for years, about going to church and about associating with companions of whom she does not approve. She has also been protected all her life and still has the bearing and the features of a child:

> [Elle avait] . . . la poitrine plate et le visage sans âge des femmes qui vieillissent avant d'avoir vécu. . . . les sangs divers dont elle a hérité n'ont pas été brassés, au cours d'une vie sans orages. Sa présence crée un malaise analogue à celui qu'on éprouve à la vue d'un organisme inachevé, qui se flétrit avant d'avoir mûri. (16)

Before her marriage her family had enough money to live comfortably, and her husband has always provided for her economically and sheltered her from life.

At the time of the opening of the novel she is still a petulant child, as seen in her reaction to going to the wedding: "Elle crispa ses doigts sur le dossier du fauteuil: 'Je ne veux pas, cria-t-elle, je ne veux pas'" (44). This is echoed by Eugène-Marie at the wedding when he tells his uncle that he has decided to do in life exactly what he wants and nothing else; his uncle replies that he had decided the same thing when he was young. Twenty years later Eugène-Marie's mother lives with him and his wife just as his maternal grandfather had lived with his family when he was young. Her face has become "pétrifié . . . dans une expression crispée," her hair and her skin are gray, and she still has her little girl's voice and "un regard égaré" (217-18). The housekeeper describes her as being morally thirteen years old. Domenica takes care of her and has compassion on her, saying that she was made to live in more tranquil times. Eugène-Marie's paternal grandmother, Eugénie, answers that times are never tranquil. She is thus seen as the end product of a life of protection and coddling; trying to keep an unsoiled purity leads to stunted growth and a loss of "élan vital."

Michel Favart, Eugène-Marie's father, also wants to protect him from life, to keep him "à l'abri des batailles de la vie" (61). He is an "ingénieur," which actually means a surveyor and cartographer. He has lived his life by taking as few risks as possible and opting at every opportunity for security rather than adventure. He enjoys his work, which he considers an adventure, but his wife continually nags him for having settled for "des professions en marge, dans des situations de second ordre" (20). He wears glasses: "La myopie et les binocles caractérisaient à cette époque les professions libérales; ils étaient l'apanage des intellectuels dont les épouses disaient fièrement: *il ne sait rien faire de ses mains, il ne faut pas lui en vouloir; il vit dans la lune*" (48). Eugène-Marie decides that his father without his glasses has "le regard doux" and that he is "doux" when left alone in his study to do as he pleases. Eugène-Marie thinks his father has the calm and attentive look of a worker, "un menuisier, qui travaillerait des bois tendres, avec des outils qui ne coupent pas" (49). He decides that his father is not good, but weak; however, they enjoy doing mathematics together, especially geometry, and Eugène-Marie is proud of him because he belongs to an elite, because he is:

> un homme dont le métier n'est ni de fabriquer, ni de vendre, ni d'acheter, qui n'est pas dans les affaires, mais qui n'a quand même pas de patron, qui est à son compte, comme on dit, qui ne touche ni salaire, ni appointements, ni commissions, ni gratifications, mais des honoraires: tel est le privilège des professions libérales. (65)

When they talk together about Eugène-Marie's plans for the future, his father tries to persuade him to be a professor so he can have an "assured career" and vacations to devote himself to pure mathematics or poetry or whatever he wants to do, but Eugène-Marie intends to go to the École Polytechnique or Centrale and be an engineer. Although he has already reached "l'âge de la raison" and is an atheist, Eugène-Marie does not blame his father too much for going to church the past few years even though he was a freemason; he excuses him by seeing in his church attendance a gesture, the only kind possible for this man "qui ne quitte jamais ses binocles, n'est jamais monté sur un vélo, qui ne va pas au café, qui ne regarde pas la poitrine des femmes et qui ne sait pas parler aux hommes" (67). Eugène-Marie remembers an old man who had stalked out of a first communion service, protesting that he simply could not stay; Eugène-Marie had admired him because he had not blushed, but he does not think he would have liked for his father to be the one who caused such a scandal. Militant anticlericalism seems to Eugène-Marie just like politics, political newspapers, and speeches at the awards ceremonies at school; his father had never voted, and Eugène-Marie finds this quite "natural."

At the wedding he is introduced to all kinds of political beliefs, fervor, and disillusionment, but everyone is vitally interested one way or another. As to his father's gesture of going to church, his uncle Lucien explains to him that his father is doing what everyone else in a world where there is no longer any security or any morality is doing, trying to hide. Although Eugène-Marie is repelled by the "gauloiserie" of most of the guests at the wedding, he is humiliated by his father's obvious discomfort and awkwardness in their presence and tries to act so as not to be identified with him.

His father's model is, thus, not one which he would want to follow, but he has been exposed to no others. Because of his mother's dislike of his paternal grandmother, he hears at the wedding for the first time stories about his grandfather, who left family tradition and his studies for the priesthood in order to join the army of Napoleon III, left that army to join the Communards, and later made a fortune with a large chain of restaurants. It would seem that this grandfather possessed the character, courage, and ability to adapt to circumstances which would make of him a heroic model to be emulated. However, Eugène-Marie finds out that his uncle Lucien had taken this man, his father, and his teachings as a model, that his father had taken him to political meetings and had taught him to be ambitious for others and for himself. His father never completely recovered from the wound he received fighting in the Commune and rarely left the house: "Il se contentait de semer des espoirs déraisonnables dans le coeur de ceux qui l'entouraient" (128). He thus can be compared to the wounded Lamballe looking down from his mountain; too great a distance can lead to distortion and optical illusions. Because of the influence of his father, Lucien became an ardent socialist, anti-militarist, and pacifist, only to be sent off to war by a government in which the socialists participated, leaving him completely disillusioned and disgusted with himself and with others. He tells Eugène-Marie that when he is a little more "avachi," he will probably return to the socialist party because treason is the most lucrative way to "se défendre." The investigation in Part II reveals that he did return to politics, joined the Pétain government, and became a cabinet director of the Minister of Labor. His life can thus be seen as a warning against too little distance, against giving oneself completely to something without viewing it critically.

In contrast to Eugène-Marie, who wants to reject his father's model, and to Lucien, whose model was a wounded ex-combattant, young Jacques Madru in Part II has as his model his father Pierre Madru, the perfect husband, father, train engineer, and "vrai bolchevik," who, far from trying to shelter his son or to inspire him with past exploits, takes him in as a comrade in arms in the Resistance. Only time will tell the outcome of the struggle and the reaction of Jacques to whatever happens. The young Eugène-Marie finds his models in literature, especially in Corneille and Stendhal. One of his professors has introduced him to Rimbaud, in whom he particularly admires the adventurer and his condemnation of society, but his favorite work remains Le Cid.

Un Jeune Homme Seul is structured around three "gifles." The first occurred in 1899 when Eugénie Favart slapped her son Michel because he had failed the examination to enter the École Polytechnique. This slap, "reçue et acceptée à l'âge de dix-neuf ans" (18), had influenced the rest of his life because rather than risk another failure Michel had entered a Ministry of Agriculture competition, thus beginning his career as surveyor. This slap has been present throughout the childhood of Eugène-Marie because his mother speaks of it continually and calls every action of Eugénie Favart another slap. Eugène-Marie repeatedly compares himself to his father, asks himself what he would have done in his father's place, and tries to imagine how it would feel to be slapped. He decides: "Une gifle exige du sang" (50) and "moi j'ai du coeur" (51). He proves this to himself when, being beaten by his father, he turns on his tormentor calling him a coward and threatening to strike him when he is older. The second slap occurs at the end of Part I when Eugène-Marie is trying, very crudely, to "avoir" Marcelle. She slaps him twice, and he has his fist raised to hit her when Madru stops him, saying: "Tu ne sais donc pas qu'on ne se bat pas avec une femme" (138). Madru understands that he is still a child, but he tells him: "Une gifle fait voir rouge . . . . Mais cette gifle-là, tu l'avais bien cherchée" (139). At this time Eugène-Marie wants to run after Madru, to talk to him, but instead he returns to his "maison particulière." The exploitative, individualistic nature of his conception of honor, of the "homme de coeur," remains untempered by "le coeur" or by any experience in the real world. The third slap occurs at the end of Part II when Inspector Marchand slaps Jacques Madru and Eugène-Marie "voit rouge," not because of a slap given to himself, but to one of "les siens," thus ending his long solitude. But just as the scene with Marcelle was the culmination of many frustrations, so this is the culmination of many experiences and influences.

Although he has no living models to follow as a child and no environmental influences to help him, he does have the same blood as his grandmother and grandfather Favart. His grandfather died shortly after his birth, and he rarely sees his grandmother, but Godichaux, his maternal grandfather, tells him he is "fait du même bois" as his grandmother Favart, whereas his sister Béatrice does not seem to be "du même sang" (27). His mother tells him his stubbornness is not his fault because it comes from his Favart blood (39). Traboulaz, president of the Savoyards in Rheims, recognizes him as a Favart and adds: "Les Savoyards sont faits pour courir les chantiers . . . . Ça leur réussit mieux que de gratter le papier" (56). At the wedding everyone agrees that his Favart blood has won out over the Godichaux. Madru's opinion is: "C'est un gosse, mais je ne crois pas que ce soit un mauvais gosse. . . . Il est de bon sang" (139). Twenty years later La Blanchette tells the inspector that she became the lover of the young Eugène-Marie because, although he was timid, shy, and repressed, he had the same "qualités de coeur" as his grandmother (192).

Eugénie Favart is evidently the kind of person Albéran would have been if he had been born in another time. Eugène-Marie's first thoughts of her are of her intransigence and her grandeur, but it becomes obvious that what he calls intransigence is not rigidity, but an ability to remain herself and to redefine herself in relation to circumstances. His grandfather Godichaux describes her in her prime as "orgueilleuse comme un roi" and explains what he means:

> Les rois disaient: _nous voulons_, pour bien nous faire comprendre qu'ils voulaient à notre place; le peuple n'avait pas le droit de vouloir; le peuple n'avait qu'à se taire; la volonté du peuple, c'était ce que voulait la volonté du roi. Voilà pourquoi le roi disait: _nous voulons_. Eh bien! Eugénie Favart disait toujours: nous voulons. (24)

This was at the height of her power when she had "ses titres à elle, à son nom . . . cotés en bourse" (23), but after the money was lost in the crash of the Say Refineries, she started saying "je" rather than "nous." Godichaux says that at the time he and she were "les meilleurs," but whereas he, after losing his fortune because of the Russian Revolution, lost also his self-respect, came to live with his daughter, and accepted being treated like a servant, Eugénie sold her house, took an apartment in a working-class neighborhood, set up an antique shop, and finally bowed to necessity and gave a splendid wedding for her son and a girl of the working class.

At the time of the wedding she is described as "Droite comme une jeune fille, _du temps que les jeunes filles savaient encore se tenir_, cheveux teints en noir, joues passées au rouge, elle ne paraît pas quarante-cinq ans; elle a dépassé les soixante-cinq" (81). Domenica tells Eugène-Marie that her father said that Eugénie was "une femme de fer, qu'elle serait digne d'être espagnole" (92). Twenty years later she is a "Gaulliste enragée" who has not been arrested because she is over eighty years old and is considered harmless by the police. She appears just when she is needed most and takes charge. She is at this time identified as the ancestor: "L'aïeule avait maintenant les cheveux blancs. Mais elle se tenait aussi droite que vingt ans plus tôt" (221). In _Les Pléïades_, the ancestor can be separated by many generations from the "fils de roi," but a closer relationship is used in this novel so that the quality of the ancestor can be seen. She says of herself: "J'ai plus de quatre-vingts ans, je ne demande rien à personne, et c'est encore moi qui aide les autres" (229). She has "confiance" in Eugène-Marie because "il est de bon sang" (229).

In addition to the ancestor, Eugène-Marie in Part II has also the love of Domenica, who at the time of the wedding in Part I taught him that fighting for liberty can be a family tradition and that prisons do not enclose only criminals. At age thirteen she was already learning to shoot and planned to get a degree in law and in sciences at the same time in order to be prepared for the fight, saying: "Est-ce que j'ai une tête à mourir dans mon lit?" (90). Twenty years later she is described as she cleans the kitchen:

> Ses gestes étaient précis comme les pas d'une danseuse. Elle ne demandait jamais l'aide de personne pour planter un clou, tenait le marteau entre trois doigts, et calculait d'instinct la multiplication de la force par le levier avec tant de justesse, qu'elle enfonçait la pointe en trois coups sans faire de bruit. (219)

This compares with the iron fists of Madru, which on the throttle of a locomotive become "sa main habile à toute chose, sensible et juste comme une bonne balance" (230); both descriptions contrast with the myopic intellectual who does not know how to do anything with his hands. Domenica is a woman who "s'occupe de son intérieur," who patiently picks up after and cares for her mother-in-law, who loves Eugène-Marie in the good times, "toujours à s'embrasser, par-ci par-là, et à roucouler comme des jeunes mariés" (170), and who cares for him in his periods of crisis: "Elle le regarde avec ses grands yeux tendres, comme une mère qui a accouché d'un infirme," firmly convinced that one day "il guérira" (171). Madru also had "le regard tendre et maître de soi-même" (231), which obviously contrasts with "le regard doux" of Michel Favart.

This tender, loving woman has been a Communist since 1934, has been working in the Resistance with Madru, and briefly takes over the role as leader after his death. She also shows good judgment in that she does not tell Eugène-Marie of her activities because she knows that he is not ready. Her family background stands her in good stead during her interrogation by the inspector: "Mon père a passé sa vie à combattre pour la liberté du peuple espagnol; aucune saleté d'aucune police ne peut étonner une Dominguez" (208). She tells him nothing not even when he explains that freeing her will be proof to her comrades that she has given him information: "Vous avez fait preuve de caractère. Logiquement, à perdre l'estime de vos camarades, à l'excommunication, vous devez préférer les tortures de la Gestapo et la mort" (216). He mistakenly assumes that she is fighting because she is a Communist, when she actually is a Communist because they are fighting for the same thing she has always been fighting for. She tells Eugénie that times have changed: "Aujourd'hui on ne peut plus transformer sa maison tout seul. C'est le monde dont il faut changer la face, avec l'aide de tous les hommes de bonne volonté" (229). She has "confiance" in Eugène-Marie because "il aspire à la fraternité des hommes" (229).

But Eugène-Marie at the beginning of Part II is still living in his "maison particulière," which he describes to the inspector as a villa:

> Mais regardez où elle est placée: elle ouvre sur l'avenue de la Gare et mon jardinet est fermé par une grille de fer de lance; mais elle touche par derrière à la cité ouvrière et le mur de mon potager est mitoyen avec le mur du potager des hommes d'équipe. (188)

He is in a no-man's land; even though he is not rich, the poor will have nothing to do with him. The investigation reveals that he did try to become different from his father and more like his Savoyard ancestors. He rejected the safe teaching career envisioned by his father by receiving an engineer's degree from the École Centrale des Arts et Manufactures, but he fulfilled the expectations of his class by thus becoming part of the elite of professional cadres. After the death of his father following the American stock market crash in 1929, he and a friend with a rich mother bought a small printing business, enlarged it, and branched out into luxury editions. During this time he lived in a room above the shop, and, leaving all the commercial affairs to his friend, he "composait, tirait, rognait, pliait, empaquetait, il avait appris tous les métiers de l'imprimerie et les pratiquait tous; il balayait même la boutique" (183). The business, ill-fated from the beginning because it was a case of trying to do the wrong thing at the wrong time, did allow him to do what he wanted to do despite the rest of the world and to prove that he, unlike his father, could work with his hands. The business and his relationship with La Blanchette, an older woman who, unknown to him, was also engaging in prostitution, both emphasized his solitude and his separation from the world of his time.

In his job as chief of the railroad yard, he is salaried and experiences regular end-of-the-month financial difficulties. He is considered by the director of personnel as a "brillant ingénieur," who handles his job competently and as unobstrusively as possible. Speaking to the inspector for the first time, he is very correct, using his position and "l'habitude des chefs de service," as rationale for his actions. He remains strictly within the rules; as Roncevaux tells the inspector: "Madru et moi, nous lui avons demandé dix fois de nous aider, il a toujours refusé. Il n'a même pas voulu fermer les yeux" (178). The bartender says of him: "Mais même quand il est plein, il garde toujours de la tenue. C'est vraiment ce qu'on appelle un homme bien élevé" (164).

This façade, however, hides problems. He has periods during which he drinks every night in working-class bars, one of the things he wanted to do at the wedding: "Il va prendre l'apéritif sur le zinc, dans un bistrot d'ouvriers, comme si c'était la chose la plus naturelle. Il va enfin 'faire comme tout le monde'" (85). He did not go then when invited because he felt too embarrassed by what he considered his stupidity and instead returned to his room lamenting his solitude. Now every night he buys a round of drinks for the workers, calling them "tu," and then pays no attention to them, but drinks steadily, his head in his hands, "partie du décor" (159). During these periods of crisis, he has what Domenica calls "les réveils pénibles de mon mari" (170), recalling Milan's stories of his early life in the working world and Antoinette's life while working at the laboratory. Staying in bed past the time to get up, reminded several times by Domenica that it is late, he finally calls her into the room and begins to lament: "Je n'ai pas plus de raison pour me lever que pour rester couché; un jour je me tirerai une balle dans la tête, pour ne pas avoir à choisir." (169). During these complaints, he shows his dissatisfaction with his life and his ambivalence toward solitude, wanting to live alone, but hating his "maison particulière." His disgust with himself and with others is shown in his reported outburst at Madru in a bar: "Ce sont des salauds, les uns comme les autres. Moi aussi je suis un salaud. Mais je préfère rester tout seul, salaud dans ma saloperie" (164).

The dangers of complete disillusionment with no hope of heroes and the possibility of the solidification of the façade are illustrated by La Blanchette and a conversation Eugène-Marie had years earlier with her. Speaking of prostitution, she said that she was actually harming no one and that it was just as good a way as any to make a living. She had a pimp because that was one of the rules of the game, but she really wanted to live in peace with her daughter. She turned her pimp over to the police, sent him money in prison every month, and was not bothered by anyone. She insisted, however, that she was a slut: "Si je n'étais pas une salope, je ne ferais pas la putain" (200).

When Eugène-Marie tried to defend her : "Ce n'est pas ton métier que je te reproche . . . . Tu n'as pas eu de chance, tu te débrouilles comme tu peux, tu mérites autant de respect qu'une femme mariée qui n'aime pas son mari" (200), she replied that he did not know what he was talking about and what she submitted to in her work: "Il y a des chevaux vicieux, des chiens sournois, des taureaux qui refusent de se battre, des hommes lâches, et des femmes qui ne valent rien. Moi, je ne vaux rien" (200). There is thus a return to the position of Marat in Drôle de Jeu that there are things or actions which in themselves are absolutely humiliating and degrading. This is the position which Milan and Roberte tried to deny throughout their marriage, but which both of them finally accepted. It is the position denied by the prostitutes and by Rodrigue in Bon Pied Bon Oeil.

La Blanchette's lack of respect for herself or for others is represented by and reflected in her face and her bearing; she had no wrinkles, but her face was:

> immobile comme la pierre, avec deux traits courts, comme creusés au ciseau . . . ce sont les plis de l'humiliation consentie. . . . Elle se tenait . . . comme l'une des colonnes sans frise ni chapiteau, faite d'un seul bloc de basalte, qui soutiennent les temples très anciens de la Haute-Égypte. (201)

The petrification of Eugène-Marie's mother was caused by a refusal to face life and to develop organically; la Blanchette's was caused by facing it, becoming completely disillusioned with it and with herself, and then refusing further growth or development. This is the danger for Lamballe in his environment of solidified lava and for Eugène-Marie, who has a low opinion of himself and of others. He does, however, respect the workers and would like to be accepted by them. He explains to the inspector that he did not join Madru because he disliked being asked to fulfill a duty as a Frenchman rather than to do something for a comrade. He refused because he would still be alone. His grandmother tells Domenica this attitude is childish: "Ce sont les enfants qui ont besoin d'être cajolés pour faire ce qu'ils doivent faire" (228). But he does not have to be cajoled to attend Madru's funeral. He comes unasked to take his place with Eugénie, Domenica, and Jeanne Madru at the head of the funeral procession because: "Madru . . . est le seul homme au monde que j'ai jamais respecté" (226). This act, like that of the shopworkers in 1936 discussed in Drôle de Jeu, unveils the new man or the one who was there all the time in the process of coming into being. When the cortege enters the main avenue under the eyes of the police and timid bourgeois peeping from behind the curtains, as Eugène-Marie had done in his youth, and in front of all the people gathered to pay hommage to Madru: "Favart se redressa, ses bras s'allongèrent le long du corps, le cou se raidit, le pas devint aisé, ample et un peu solennel, et plus personne ne s'étonna qu'il fût en tête de tous, le premier des hommes de la famille" (230). Thus the act of paying respect imparts self-respect.

The opening scene of the novel presents the young Eugène-Marie coming home on his bicycle congratulating himself on the good time he has made and the good form he is in. He is so engrossed in "son style" that he does not see approaching from the opposite direction a worker, who has to swerve sharply to avoid hitting Eugène-Marie, causing damage to his bicycle and cutting his forehead. Eugène-Marie's delight in style and workmanship is reemphasized by a scene told by La Blanchette about the days when he had the print shop and was producing luxury editions. Working on the title page of a surrealist work, he is asked by La Blanchette what he is printing. He answers: "Je ne sais pas . . . mais je crois que je n'ai jamais réussi une mise en pages aussi élégante" (196).

In Part II the character who shares his interest in style and elegance is the sadistic Vichy inspector, and the confrontations between the two of them furnish Eugène-Marie with a negative model in many ways like that of La Blanchette. The inspector points out to him the similarity between Eugène-Marie's interest in mathematics and his own in music and adds that they have in common:

> que vous avez rêvé de consacrer votre vie aux mathématiques pures et que vous passez le plus clair de votre temps à rédiger des rapports sur les accidents survenus dans le cuvelage des plaques tournantes; que j'ai rêvé d'écrire des symphonies et que je suis devenu policier. (174-75)

He has succeeded in using music in his "triste métier" through his theory that each man plays his own tune all his life, and that apparent discords are only fragments of a counterpoint which he has not yet recognized:

> Alors, je me joue l'air de mon client, j'essaie des contrepoints, je tâtonne; c'est là que l'artiste intervient. Quand j'ai trouvé le contrepoint qui rend leur sens à toutes les dissonances, je sais tout ce que je veux savoir du passé et du présent de mon client. Je peux méme prédire son avenir; je n'ai qu'à continuer à jouer dans le ton. (175)

The inspector's clients, are, of course, human beings whom he is attempting to arrest so they can be imprisoned, tortured, or killed. He sees his work, just as Eugène-Marie saw his bicycle riding, as divided into three stages: observation, experimentation (interrogation), and execution. He sees his work as an end in itself no matter who is using it: "Les nouvelles autorités m'utiliseront contre les anciennes, ma technique est la seule dont aucun régime ne peut se passer" (212); it is just like a game of chess with people's lives as pawns: "Une enquête de trente-six heures, trois conversations, un peu de réflexion, je place mes pièces, échec et mat, l'exécution est impeccable, je n'ai jamais travaillé aussi élégamment" (214). He works only for himself and the satisfaction he derives from the work: "Je ne m'intéresse ni à mon gouvernement ni à ceux qu'il me fait exécuter. Seule m'importe la rigueur et l'élégance de l'exécution. . . . Moi je suis un artiste" (215).

Like Lucien, who had said that he might as well marry Lucie as anyone else since all women are alike, Inspector Marchand thinks all human beings are alike because all his clients end up "par se mettre à table" and that all men are equal "devant le policier, comme devant le médecin et le confesseur" (242). Eugène-Marie, after the experience of Madru's funeral, knows this is not true and insists that Madru would have told him nothing. The inspector makes the mistake of thinking that Eugène-Marie is "un homme raisonnable," who respects only "le beau tableau noir où vous écrivez si vite vos interminables équations" (243). Jacques Madru escapes through the efforts of Eugène-Marie, who goes to prison to discover fraternal tenderness, while Domenica, without communicating with her husband, cycles toward Eugénie and the fight for liberty with a Gaullist group.

Thus within the first four novels can be seen a definite repudiation of any ethical aestheticism based on exploitation of others and of literary aestheticism which is its own end. There is also a repudiation of an individual life style based on the idea of adventure for its own sake or on a romantic ideal of heroism or love which ignores the facts of daily life, but there is a recognition of the apparent need for heroes of some kind. Critical examination of self and of others is seen as a necessity in order to understand past experience and present actions and reactions. Reason, in order to make valid judgment, must be accompanied by a wide range of experiences and must not be satisfied with abstractions. The ever-present power of the printed word, especially that word that creates fictional characters, is quite evident, as is the seemingly human penchant to seek role models in life and in literature. Equality is seen as an empty concept, whereas quality is seen to exist in real life: some things and some people are worth more than others. The search for place in society has not ended, but at this point it is evident that this place must be with other people of quality, worthy of respect and capable of acting in the world.

THE ACTIVE WITNESS

In *Un Jeune Homme Seul*, Vailland had to return to a time of war to find a black-and-white situation where Lamballe's position was no longer tenable. Once that situation had been clarified, the atmosphere of the Korean War and specifically the arrest of Jacques Duclos in 1952 followed literature and furnished the situation. Lamballe in *Bon Pied Bon Oeil* attended the wedding of Antoinette and Rodrigue, and Antoinette commented on the fact that he was their witness. In *Beau Masque*, published in 1954, and *325.000 francs*, published the following year, Vailland appears writing in the first person as a character who is intended to be himself, called Roger in *Beau Masque* and with no name except "je" in *325.000 francs*. In the made-for-television movie of the latter novel, Vailland played the part of himself. In both these novels the primary focus is a working-class milieu with which the author has a relationship. He bears witness to that milieu and to the relationship.

The events in *Beau Masque* (entitled *Pierrette Amable* in translations in Communist countries) take place in a mountain village, La Grange-aux-Vents, and in the small textile town of Le Clusot below it in the valley; the events occur from March through October 195., but a brief epilogue recounts the situation a year later. The novel is a description and analysis of the economic situation of the area, including the small farmers of La Grange-aux-Vents, exemplified by Pierrette's uncle Aimé Amable, who are being squeezed out of business by large cooperatives or corporations and by the worn-out land. The principal industry of the area is the textile mill of Le Clusot, once a large family enterprise, but now owned by a company called F.E.T.A (Filatures et Tissages

Anonymes). The novel unmasks the anonymous people who run the company and shows how their actions influence the daily lives of the inhabitants of Le Clusot. In the beginning the workers know nothing about the power structure of the company, their only experience being with Noblet, the personnel director, and Tallagrand, the technical director, who are also ignorant as to who really has ultimate authority in the organization. By the end of the novel Pierrette herself has been to Lyons to meet Northemaire, the regional director; Noblet has been to the home of Valerio Empoli, one of the principal stockholders, and has talked to him; the principal stockholders have been to Le Clusot; and the workers are able to situate their mill and their work in an international framework with the confidence that people like them all over the world are doing the same.

The action revolves around Beau Masque, a former welder at the shipbuilding yards of Ansaldo in Genoa, who, because of a wartime act, is wanted by the Italian police. While his friends in Italy are working with lawyers to set matters straight, he is living in Le Clusot, collecting milk from the peasants and delivering it to the cooperative. Pierrette Amable, a divorcee with a small child, works at the knitting mill and is a militant Communist. She is admired by Beau Masque and by Philippe Letourneau, grandson of "le grand Letourneau" who really made the mill a big business. Philippe, who knows and cares nothing about the business, is nominal director of personnel at the mill in Le Clusot at the behest of his mother Émilie Empoli, now the wife of Valerio Empoli, a wealthy banker. Émilie is attempting to gain control of the stock of the company for her and her American friends; if she succeeds, she will divorce Valerio and marry a wealthy American.

Nourishing a fantasized love for Pierrette and wishing to gain her respect and that of the workers, Philippe takes Noblet to Lyons to protest the proposed change in the mills, a change which would increase production and occasion the dismissal of half the workers. Valerio suggests setting up only one room with the new changes and having a grand opening as a media event to impress the Americans who are thinking of investing in the mill and as a means of firing only a few of the workers. Activity begins immediately to implement this plan, opposed by the workers. As a result of Philippe's visit Émilie goes to see Pierrette, offering to take her to America with her. Pierrette is insulted when she realizes that Émilie thinks she is Philippe's mistress, but Beau Masque, with whom she has had a pleasant sexual experience, comes in just in time for her to identify him to Émilie as "mon amant."

Pierrette and Beau Masque set up housekeeping together with disastrous results for both of them. He, emprisoned by his own stereotypes of male dominance, feels insecure in his marginal position in Le Clusot and, goaded on by Philippe, becomes increasingly jealous of Pierrette's activities and of her co-workers. She begins to be trapped by domestic life and by pregnancy. Plans go forward, without much enthusiasm, for a planned demonstration on the day of the grand opening of the new knitting room. Valerio Empoli, wishing to thwart his wife's plans, makes sure the workers receive through Philippe newspapers clarifying the situaion and what is really happening; in addition, he is responsible for firing forty percent of the workers a few days before the opening, uniting the workers as nothing else could. Pierrette and the other delegates call a general strike, and everyone is excited about the day of the demonstration. Pierrette, caught up in the excitement and knowing of Beau Masque's jealousy, lies to him about her companion during a speaking engagement to a neighboring town. Knowing that she is lying because he spied on her, he is about to beat her when the police come to arrest her, having decided that the leaders should be in jail the day of the demonstration. On that day, the demonstration takes place without the leaders, and Beau Masque and Vazille, an individualistic old hero, use fire hoses to destroy the exhibition tents. When the police arrive, Vazille is able to jump into the river and escape, but Beau Masque chooses to remain and is killed. Philippe, thinking the others are coming to accuse him of driving Beau Masque to suicide, kills himself, and Pierrette, having escaped from jail, convinces Vazille that an individualistic, heroic revenge for Beau Masque would only harm the Party. For the immediate present, Émilie's plans have been thwarted and the proposed changes in the mill stopped.

In the beginning of the novel the author writes that he came to La Grange-aux-Vents after a long trip beyond Java and Bali to write about that trip, evidently considering the locale to be a safe retreat in which to write. In the beginning he kept a journal in which he wrote his impressions: "Le lecteur trouvera ci-dessus quelques-unes de ces notes. Les faits sont exactement relatés. Beaucoup de mes jugements durent être révisés par la suite" (10). The changes in his original judgments and the fact that he abandoned the journal after six weeks reflect his increasing involvement with the people and the events of the novel. His position in the beginning is similar to that of Lamballe: "De la place de l'église, en terrasse au-dessus d'une gorge sauvage où gronde un torrent, on domine de fort haut la plaine toujours brumeuse où la rivière d'Ain s'unit au Rhône" (9) and that of Eugène-Marie in Rheims:

> Je peux tour à tour plonger le regard dans la cour d'Ernestine et de Justin . . . et dans celle des Amable . . . . Mes fenêtres surplombent les deux perrons, et, à l'abri des rideaux, je surprends tout à l'aise ce qui se passe dans l'une et l'autre salle commune. (10)

He makes clear that he does not see them by accident, but that he is, in fact, a voyeur: "Tout à l'heure j'ai soulevé un coin de mes rideaux pour regarder dans cette pale clarté" (13).

But he is not, like Eugène-Marie, simply a spectator imprisoned behind the curtains; he has a broader perspective, as evidenced by his voyage, and he has a life where he is well known: "La presse locale a signalé mon arrivée dans la région et un reporter de Grenoble est venu m'interroger sur mes projets littéraires et politiques" (12). He also has human contacts which Eugène-Marie did not have; catching rides to and from the train station with Beau Masque, he accompanies him on his rounds. The author once wrote an article about a strike at Ansaldo and can talk about riveting with Beau Masque. They are soon on a first-name basis, and the author makes clear that it is from Beau Masque himself that he gets information for the introduction to the character:

> C'est ainsi que Beau Masque fut amené à me raconter sa vie. Cela se fit d'une semaine à l'autre, au cours de nos voyages. Pour simplifier, je vais en dire tout d'un trait les événements dont la connaissance est nécessaire à la compréhension de ce récit. (21)

The second chapter relates the events at a community dance which the author attended in the town of Le Clusot, but includes events which he did not observe. He explains at the beginning of the chapter how he knows what was going on: "Quelques mois plus tard, quand les événements nous eurent rapprochés, Nathalie Empoli . . . me raconta l'enchaînement de circonstances qui l'avait amenée, elle aussi, au bal du Clusot, et comment la soirée s'était déroulée pour elle" (35). It is also from Nathalie, the daughter of Valerio and the step-sister of Philippe, that he gets, according to him, her correspondence with Philippe. He gives indications throughout the novel as to how he gathered his information: "Je n'étais pas à la Grange-aux-Vents ce dimanche-là, et ce ne fut que peu à peu, par les confidences de Beau Masque, de Pierrette et de Mignot, que j'appris comment s'était déroulée la journée" (167). He thus has human relationships with people who are willing to confide in him. During the summer he comes back briefly to Le Clusot: "J'allai tout naturellement frapper chez Pierrette" (289). They invite him to stay for supper, and Beau Masque calls him "notre ami."

He also fulfills in their lives, and they in his, a function that is not just that of a friend. At the dance sponsored by the Communist Party, he is seated at the table with the members of the section committee and their families, indicating that he is a "comrade" in addition to being a friend. Mignot, the section secretary, brings him documents for possible use in "des articles de journaux" (97), and he does become interested enough to embark on a series of articles devoted to the textile industry, which he has almost completed by the end of the novel. It is through the author's research for these articles that he succeeds in proving the American connection with the French textile industry. He helps the strike committee write a new tract to be distributed at the demonstration after Pierrette asks for his aid: "C'est ton métier" (375). It is not as a voyeur, but as a fellow participant in the action that he observes Pierrette and comes to understand her: "Puis elle sourit. Je fus étourdi de la bonté de ce sourire. Ce fut de ce jour-là et dans cet instant que je commençai à comprendre Pierrette Amable" (373). The day of the demonstration he and a reporter are in an upstairs window overlooking the exhibition tents: "Nous préparions nos articles, en suivant les événements de derrière les rideaux" (416-17). Events and his involvement in them have changed the perspective from behind the curtains, and watching from behind the curtains is his place in this particular action.

The author is thus vitally involved in the events, both from the human standpoint and from that of his "métier." He is not imprisoned in the town and on the land as some of the characters feel that they are; neither is he a "promeneur solitaire" because he has a role to fill in the novel, a role which requires that he be mobile and have a larger perspective. The broadening of perspective, finding one's place in the real world and situating that place in a larger framework, thus enhancing a sense of self-respect are the major themes of the novel, experienced by Nathalie, the author, Pierrette, and the workers in Le Clusot "avec leur volonté passionnée de ne pas se tromper, de ne plus se tromper, de ne plus être trompés" (435). Philippe and Beau Masque have the opposite experience of a rigidity or narrowing of perspective, failure to find a place, and loss of self-respect, resulting from self-deception, deception by others, or both.

When the action is completed, the author writes the novel, unveiling the truth so others will not be deceived in the future. The first four novels were, in great part, instruments enabling the author to clarify--for himself principally and only incidentally for others-- himself and his relation to other people and to certain specific problems so that he could be certain that he was acting and not being acted upon. With Beau Masque it is assumed that any clarification for him occurred while the events were taking place; the novel thus becomes an instrument of clarification for the reader so that he will be able to act and not be acted upon. The novel itself is thus seen as a fraternal gesture, a gift from one comrade to another, from one human being to another. But the gift is obviously intended as a weapon, following the lead of Émilie: "Elle n'engageait jamais d'opérations sans se renseigner au préalable des positions et des forces de l'adversaire" (207).

What he presents for the reader to view is capitalism, based on personal accumulation of wealth or property achieved by ruthless exploitation of others, and the value-system accruing to it. This is seen as "la sauvagerie," as exemplified by the farmlands of La Grange-aux-Vents returning to wilderness and the domestic animals going into the forest to mate with wild animals. The savagery of industry is seen in the increasingly impersonal, dehumanized atmosphere, characterized by the contrast between the present power structure of the F.E.T.A, which uses the workers as soldiers in a tactical operation or as pawns in a game played for personal reasons, and old Letourneau: "Il se battait ferme contre nous . . . mais il ne nous méprisait pas" (42). There is the same kind of progression, or regression, in the contrast between Tallagrand, the young engineer, and Noblet, who has been in charge of the personnel for thirty years and says: "Je connais mon monde" (352). Tallagrand's office is "un bureau vitré, surélevé, comme une passerelle de navire" (337), emphasizing his alienation from the workers at the mill in the same way his wife alienates herself from all human contacts because she considers everyone in Le Clusot as beneath her station. Tallagrand is, in part, responsible for Beau Masque's death because his personal ambition and lack of experience with the populace prompted him to send in to the regional office a report on conditions in Le Clusot out of all proportion to the actual conditions, which, in turn, prompted the administrators to arrange for armed security forces the day of the grand opening. Part of Noblet's job is finding out all he can about the private lives of the workers so the administration will know how to put pressure on them, but he is, as Valerio recognizes, "dans le fond de son coeur beaucoup plus citoyen du Clusot qu'employé de la F.E.T.A" (151). He at least sees the workers as human beings: "On ne peut pas bouleverser d'un trait de plume la vie de plusieurs centaines de familles . . . . On réfléchit . . . on cherche des solutions (120), and he recognizes that the workers are actually worse off now than in the days of old Letourneau: "Les cadences que nous imposons sont trop rapides. En huit heures l'ouvrier se fatigue davantage qu'il ne le faisait en douze heures; il ne trouve plus la force de faire son jardin" (120).

Among the stockholders there is the same division between those who are humane and those who are not. Valerio Empoli, "évidemment un homme fait" (134), is the king, the Renaissance lion, belonging to the golden age in the past, and just like everyone else subject to the forces of history, over which he has no control. The problem for him, as for the other characters, is how best to respond to circumstances which he has not made. He possesses an excess of power, like Lamballe, which he never uses for offensive purposes. His tactic in business and in life is "voir venir," and he sees so well and has had so much experience that he always wins. The only reason he plays the game in the novel is that his wife initiated it, creating a situation in which he had either to win or to lose. Having entered the game, he knows exactly how much pressure to apply on which people, including two cabinet ministers, in order to win and to inflict as little damage as possible on everyone except the actual opponent. The "baie vitrée" of his dining room contrasts with the office of Tallagrand. His view of the garden for which he keeps two gardeners and spends three million a year illustrates his desire for dominance over external nature rather than over fellow human beings. It is Valerio in this novel who smiles "presque tendrement" (140). He has no illusions about big business, calling it "la dramaturgie" (231), or about life; his attitude toward mankind in general is scorn: "Mais il en était triste" (211). He tends to respect the Communists, recognizing that "Nous ne jugeons plus les événements qu'en fonction d'eux" (147). His tone is usually detached "comme s'il avait décrit de très loin un spectacle piquant et qui ne le concernait absolument pas" (147), but he does take interest in problems which circumstances lead him to study.

Nathalie quotes him as having said: "Quand on ne se suicide pas, on se doit de vivre avec tenue" (281).

His daughter Nathalie shows what he may have been like in his youth, just as he is a model for what she may someday become. She continually says that "la F.E.T.A, c'est moi"; the analogy with "L'État, c'est moi" is obvious (the fact that the Revolution is seen in an increasingly distant future explains the necessity for the kind of apprenticeship Pierrette undergoes in the novel). It turns out that Nathalie is right because her six per cent stock added to either of the opposing factions controls any vote. She is conscious of belonging to "one of the great ruling families of the world," but she has weak lungs, smokes and drinks too much, is bi-sexual, and recognizes that she has been sick all her life: "Je guérirais vite si j'avais quelque chose à faire" (227). Unlike Philippe, she understands the world and how it works and understands people and their motivations; she is mistress of her own fortune, but she writes to Philippe about his passion for Pierrette: "Moi, je ne connaîtrai jamais cela, je suis trop maîtresse de moi-même, et puis j'ai toujours ce que je veux, êtres ou choses. Qu'est-ce que je pourrais bien vouloir aujourd'hui? Voilà le problème" (248).

She recognizes that she is "une héroïne en chômage, l'époque ne m'a laissé que de retourner mes forces contre moi-même" (276). She immediately recognizes that Pierrette has "class" and that the two of them have a great deal in common. Her underwater battles with a giant stingray, which she calls the only friend worthy of her and the only thing she has ever been afraid of, illustrate for her and for the reader that for someone who has complete mastery of self the only really heroic battle is that with death. She eschews heroism, succeeds in ridding herself of her sado-masochistic relationship with her cousin Bernarde and her neo-Nazi friends--a relationship entered into only because of the dislike of solitude--and takes a cure in a sanatorium. The jockeying for power among the stockholders and the exhibition in Le Clusot finally furnish her with something amusing, if not as dangerous or as heroic as the battles with the stingray. It is she who offers to keep Pierrette at her home in Lyons until the arrest orders are rescinded and who helps the author arrange her correspondence with Philippe. One is to assume that with her father as model and given propitious circumstances she may not turn out too badly. As her father writes to her: "Seuls les plus aptes survivent. Tu guériras parce que tu es une Empoli et ma fille" (279).

Émilie Privas-Lubas-Empoli is aptly described by Valerio:

> Elle n'a ni coeur, ni sens. C'est une petite bourgeoise française, qui fait sa situation, obstinément, sans jamais regarder autre chose que le but immédiat qu'elle s'est fixé. Elle ne comprend rien à ce qui se passe dans le monde et ne s'y intéresse absolument pas. Elle s'est élevée méthodiquement dans ce qu'elle appelle l'échelle sociale, sans jamais s'apercevoir que les barreaux en sont désormais pourris. (147-48)

Valerio is attached to her because of her health and energy and because of her coldness; the fact that she is unattainable is proof that he is not absolutely all powerful, that he is not God alone in heaven, but is still human. Émilie tolerates everything her son does, although she recognizes that he has no character: "Elle s'estimait assez de caractère pour deux" (208), and she plans to make of him "un roi du monde" (208) through her marriage to the Durand de Chambord family. The futility of this kind of dynastic empire building is seen in Valerio's remarks that she is growing older and will one day be too old to "refaire carrière" with every new power which comes along and in the fact that the very characteristics which allow her to succeed in the business world make her a mother who produces the opposite characteristics in her son.

She is compared to Aimé Amable, who, on a smaller scale, has spent his life just as Émilie has with the aim of owning all the land he can get in La Grange-aux-Vents. He has cheated his friends and his own brother and now owns twenty hectares of land which is worn out, mortgaged, and which he will soon lose because he cannot persuade Pierrette to marry the young man who holds the mortgage. Aimé, by using tremendous self-control and frequent visits to barmaids in the neighboring town, succeeded in having only one son (and a frustrated wife) so he would not have to divide up the land; but the son was killed in the war. Émilie's one son commits suicide, thus ending her blood line and that of old François Letourneau, who exploited and humiliated the workers, but let himself be taken in by his paternalistic image of himself. He was so disillusioned by the actions of "his" workers in the strike of 1924 and so disgusted at himself for letting Émilie get the best of him that he has been retired ever since. Émilie, Aimé Amable, and old Letourneau thus represent the futility of acquiring wealth to pass on to another generation, but at the same time they represent the energy and single-minded purpose with which they pursue their aims, using and destroying everything and everyone in their path.

Philippe Letourneau is an example of the dangers of adolescent revolt, of the refusal to be tamed, of the futility of "saying no" without having something to "say yes" to; his life shows that saying no is simply a way of playing the other person's game passively. In his youth he received no affection from his mother, and in response to her talking to him using expressions employed in training horses: "Je décidai de ne pas me laisser dresser. Et de toujours mal me conduire, quelle que soit la manière dont on me reprendrait" (237). He is almost completely isolated in his own world of dreams and fantasies and rarely understands the world around him, but he puts up a good front, as evidenced by the author's first description of him: "Il marchait avec aisance, comme les jeunes gens qui n'ont jamais connu de patrons qu'à la table de famille. Même l'alcool ne le faisait pas vaciller, tellement il se sentait chez lui au Clusot" (67). Later developments make clear that in reality he feels at ease and at home nowhere in the world. Nathalie diagnoses his case when she says: "Il a besoin d'être guéri de tous les maux de l'époque" (279). Unlike the sons of industrialists envisioned by Milan who know all about business because they grow up hearing it discussed around the family table, Philippe never listens when business is discussed, having learned while still young how to "close himself." Like Marat he is proud of his ability to "penser à autre chose" (119) and to put a distance between himself and his surroundings.

Everything he does is a negative gesture, like those admired by the young Eugène-Marie; he takes no pleasure in his immediate environment, as evidenced by the virtual squalor in which he lives. He had his office redecorated only to protest against the avarice of the F.E.T.A and to "épater le bourgeois," in this case to upset Noblet with abstract paintings. His credentials include a baccalauréat, two "certificats de licence lettres-philosophie," and unsuccessful enterprises undertaken in each case because of a woman. Among these enterprises are a theatrical troupe trying to follow the program of Artaud's Théâtre de la Cruauté, a Yoga school, and a small publishing house. He is a poet and quotes Lautréamont to himself; the title of his slim volume of poems, _Le Roc, la Craie, le Sable_ (81), betrays his affinity with the inanimate.

He has no friends and has never had any, but during the course of the novel he confides in Nathalie and makes up a romanticized image of the two of them silimar to those which Antoinette had of her marriage to Rodrigue: "Toi et moi . . . nous sommes deux pauvres enfants, si détachés de toute espèce d'intérêts, qu'ils soient de coeur, de peau, d'argent ou de politique, qu'il ne nous reste qu'à échanger des saluts tendrement ennuyés" (243). It is her failure to fit into this image which causes him to feel that she has deceived him. He is characterized by a lack of virility, which is seen in his lack of interest in sports and in his attitude toward cars. He has always owned slow old cars, all of them sold to him by barroom acquaintances. He realized that they were cheating him, but "il estimait que c'était son style que de se faire voler de cette manière-là" (123). His acceptance of this style contributes to his low image of himself; he admits to Nathalie: "Moi, je n'ai jamais rien su faire, ni de mes doigts, ni de ma voix, ni du reste" (254).

The workers in Le Clusot, and especially Pierrette, are the first people he has ever respected because they are different, "propres" (147), and he wants to earn their esteem. However, his life so far has consisted of not knowing what the real world is like, and he is aware that he is playing a game he does not know how to play: "C'est que la politique ouvrière est un jeu très compliqué dont j'ignore les règles" (236-37). He admits that what he really wants to do is prove to himself that he is not like the "gens de ma classe" (79), but following the pattern of his life, he dramatizes and idealizes his every action, thinking how heroic he is and imagining the reactions of Pierrette and the other workers to his actions, always behaving despite himself like a "patron." He continues in his life-long habits of self-absorption; while Pierrette tries to explain to him why the project is bad for the workers, he does not listen:

> Pendant que la jeune militante me faisait son cours, je me persuadais que ma mère et Valerio m'avaient intentionnellement poussé à mal faire . . . et que tout le monde m'avait trompé . . . . Et que Pierrette Amable me méprisait à juste titre: je ne saurai jamais me conduire. (237)

He vacillates between extreme exaltation and deepest depression, between a desire to act and withdrawal into his shell at the least real or imagined setback.

Because of his passion for Pierrette, withdrawal no longer offers the solace it once did: "Le malheur est que je ne m'intéresse plus à aucun livre" (238). His "amour passion-amour idée fixe" has taken possession of him even though he realizes that it is based on his misunderstanding of Pierrette's early behavior toward him and that she does not care for him: "Je n'en suis plus maître" (245). This love illustrates Milan's definition of love as the desire to possess and be possessed: "Je la veux comme on veut une femme et aussi comme on veut une chose. Vouloir un être, singulière expression. Je veux qu'elle soit à moi, ma propriété, pouvoir user et abuser d'elle" (249). It is a love, however, which remains abstract, despite Nathalie's repeated advice to express his feelings "concrètement." He watches Pierrette and Beau Masque from afar, using words recalling Frédéric in <u>Drôle de Jeu</u> and the young Eugène-Marie watching workers from behind the curtain, and discovers "jouissances extravagantes" (246) listening to Pierrette through a closed door. Obsessed with the idea of Pierrette and of his love for her he continually rationalizes her behavior, that of Beau Masque, and that of everyone else; but he is almost always mistaken because he does not understand real people.

Because of his love for Pierrette, he decides to become better acquainted with Beau Masque so he can learn how to get rid of him. He thus experiences for the first time what he thinks is friendship: "J'éprouve pour lui ce sentiment qui m'était aussi inconnu que l'amour et que les bons auteurs nomment amitié" (259). He is as usual the supplicant; he is grateful to Beau Masque for admitting him into his friendship, which only adds to his sense of inadequacy. He does use the confidences of his "friend" to find out his weakness and wields this knowledge to destroy him, showing that he has some of his mother's talents after all. But true to his style he destroys without creating and cannot face the results of his actions. He refuses to attend any of the festivities surrounding the grand opening: "Je n'ai rien à faire dans tout cela . . . . Je ne suis ni ouvrier ni patron, il n'y a pas de place pour moi dans ce monde, etc." (407). Feeling useless, he sees deception wherever he turns; "Nathalie l'avait trahi, Pierrette avait trahi Beau Masque, et lui, il avait assassiné son seul ami" (429). The result is disgust of "son grand corps mou" and suicide.

Beau Masque, "qui s'appelle de son vrai nom Belmaschio, ce qui signifie Beau Mâle" (18), is a man who lets himself be trapped by doing even temporarily what he said he would not do and by meeting someone whom he sees as a unicorn, or in this case a heroine. He has in common with Philippe that he has said no to family tradition--in his case, a tradition dictated by economic conditions requiring the males to go to France to work as masons, sending money home to the wife and family--and that he considers himself only temporarily in Le Clusot. Unlike Philippe he knew why he said no and had something to say yes to. He explains to the author why he did not want to be a mason: "Les vaches aussi . . . sont vaches de mère en fille, et elles font toujours à peu près le même lait. Pas de progrès dans le métier de vache, pas de progrès dans le métier de maçon" (21). He has traveled widely, learning all kinds of trades, and used the war to learn the elements of mechanics and of politics. He has had experience leading others in war and in politics and has a place of his own, the shipbuilding yards of Ansaldo, where he has a job he does well and which gives him pleasure and self-esteem.

He is the antithesis of Philippe in his personality and in his dealings with the world, but it is obvious that he is a child in that, despite his experiences, he has "played" through life. He is open and natural as opposed to Philippe's closed, artificial personality; he helps other people, is respected by everyone, and spreads joy wherever he goes. Philippe writes Nathalie of Beau Masque: "Il a la manière--voilà le mot--avec les paysans, avec les moteurs, avec les femmes" (254). This manner is the result of successful experience; since the age of eleven he has marveled at the existence of women and has approached them so naturally and with so much true emotion that they never dreamed of defending themselves. It never occurs to him that a woman would refuse him, but, as the author remarks: "Il lui arrivait plus souvent d'être choisi que de choisir" (25). The ease in his manner is also a function of the fact that he does not take any of it seriously: "Je les aide à passer le temps, comme elles m'aident à passer le temps" (30). He also is at ease with himself, not having done anything he is ashamed of.

Rather than pressuring friends in Italy to speed the process so he could return to his native land, he remains in Le Clusot, caught in the cycle of the cows and the milk, worse off than the masons who come to France. They, at least, have legal work permits, which he does not have. He remains because he has the misfortune to find a heroine. He admires Pierrette because he appreciates the superhuman effort it takes to deal with the workers day in and day out and also because she is not like the other women he has known:

> Il admirait l'intrépidité et l'intégrité de Pierrette dans les combats ouvriers, et sa connaissance des livres, qu'elle lui communiquait. Il admirait aussi sa chasteté, non qu'il jugeât la chasteté bonne en soi, mais la chasteté constituait l'un des traits les plus exceptionnels, à son idée de son héroïne. (193)

It is her difference which attracts him to her, and it is her difference which makes him uncomfortable when, after they make love "naturally" in the woods, she gets up first and behaves as he has always done with other women. He then begins to analyze what happened, which he has never done with any of the other women; in fact, he actually broods, his feelings ranging from worry that he offended her to the suspicion that she was using him; it is this suspicion which brings him to her house during Émilie's visit.

He goes from one unquestioned stereotype to another; his heroine becomes "ma femme à moi," and sex, which had previously been a pleasure for him, becomes a duty: "Il mettait un point d'honneur à faire son devoir, lequel consistait, croyait-il, à la prendre quotidiennement" (296). Then begins the internal conflict between his Italian heritage of the virile male who is "maître chez soi" (87), and the suspicion that he has become a sex object: "Je ne suis bon que pour le lit. C'est moi la femme dans la maison" (273). He becomes jealous of Mignot, who is involved regularly with Pierrette in matters of vital concern to the entire town, while he continues his marginal task of collecting the milk and putters around building and painting shelves or making a toy steamship rather than the real ones he would be making at Ansaldo.

Not having anything to do in the afternoons while Pierrette is at work, he is easy prey for Philippe during their fishing excursions and increasingly frequent drinking bouts. It is not too difficult for him to believe that her yielding so easily to him perhaps indicates that she is not different, that she is just like "all" women and will perhaps yield to someone else given the right circumstances. His jealousy makes him feel ill at ease and affects all his behavior: he breaks his fishing line repairing it; he begins to dwell on the fact that he is a foreigner and sees himself as an exile. Realizing that Pierrette would not go to Italy with him, that her place is in Le Clusot, he still cannot bring himself to leave. In a drunken stupor, he, who has always marveled at and been grateful for the existence of women, tells Mignot in front of Pierrette that: "Toutes les femmes sont des salopes" (339). He does realize that Philippe's influence has something to do with his attitude; "Si j'ai été si idiot avec Pierrette, c'est un peu de ta faute. Mais je ne t'en veux pas. Tu l'as jugée au travers des femmes de ton milieu.Tu ne comprends rien aux ouvrières" (387). But when he finally discovers that she, his heroine, "l'intègre

Pierrette," has lied to him, who has always trusted everyone, he says: "Qui pourrais-je jamais croire, maintenant que tu m'as menti?" (399). Even though he is about to beat her when the police take her away, he follows them screaming: "Ma femme!" (400). On the day of the demonstration his gesture with the fire hoses is a way of vindicating his own image of himself as much as his public image. His hesitation and decision to remain are obvious to all the observers, including the author. Whether his refusal to escape represents a refusal to live in a world where he can trust no one or disgust at his own actions, it is obvious that living would necessitate changes in his way of life and outlook on life, that it would necessitate facing his illusions. Rather than doing this, he chooses to die in a glorious gesture of heroism and male virility.

Of the principal characters it is Pierrette Amable who is seen as having a future, and one to be envied. She is not a heroine, but a human being trying to live with dignity. She is in her place doing what in that place needs to be done for the good of all and learning how better to do it in the future. Her apprenticeship is seen as the fire which tempers steel. Philippe sees her as a sword: "Elle me faisait penser à une épée, elle est comme une lame d'acier, je ne peux la comparer à rien d'autre. Il y a des êtres qui sont d'une contexture toute différente de tout le reste des humains: ils raient, mais on ne peut pas les rayer" (240). The author's prediction for her in the "temps merveilleux et terribles" which were approaching is: "Elle sera d'une trempe sans égale" (436). It is the tempering process of life which Philippe and Beau Masque had both avoided, Philippe absolutely and Beau Masque in his relationship to women. The author also sees her as an example of elegance: "L'élégance exprime des rapports intrinsèques à l'être vivant dans son unité et dans son individualité" (308). In this sense elegance is seen as the opposite of alienation. In addition to being elegant, "elle a de la race, au sens où le disent les amateurs de chevaux" (308). She thus possesses "quality," which she proved before the beginning of the novel by throwing out her husband after discovering that he was a spy and an informer for management.

In contrast to Philippe and Beau Masque, Pierrette has accepted the work of her parents, who also worked at the F.E.T.A, but she has said no to the way they approached that work. Her childhood memories are of the humiliations of her father, but rather than rejecting him or the work, she tries to change the conditions under which that work takes place, thus changing her relationship to it. She is secretary of the local C.G.T., member of the Communist Party section committee, and delegate from her shop in negotiations with management. All her life and even the first few times she was a delegate, going to see "la direction" was associated with a sense of anguish, which she no longer has because her experience has dissipated her fear and because she now goes to work like a soldier going into battle. She considers her actions in light of the way they will affect her ability to wage this battle. Refusing to dance with Philippe, she says to Mignot: "Comment veux-tu que je défende demain matin les intérêts de mes camarades contre le directeur du personnel si je rigole ce soir avec lui?" (68). When called into Philippe's office, she insists upon leaving after a short time because people might talk. Philippe cannot understand why she cares what Noblet thinks, but she answers: "J'ai besoin de son respect pour me battre à égalité avec lui" (80).

When the others are angry enough or humiliated enough, it is to her that they come for help because they like her and because they have confidence in her. She realizes: "Il ne suffit pas d'être un communiste discipliné et de répéter les 'mots d'ordre' pour entraîner les masses. Il faut avoir fait la preuve qu'on a le coeur ferme. Elle se réjouit d'avoir toujours eu le coeur ferme" (353). Never doubting that she has this modified version of "le coeur," which now involves perseverance in maintaining a certain quality in a day-by-day battle, she has made for herself a second nature, the technique of dealing with problems: "Après la détermination de la tâche, la désignation du responsable. Ensuite, il faudra 'rendre compte.' C'était devenu chez elle une seconde nature" (88).

Her courage, her experience, her familiarity with the local situation, and her judgment are qualities which enable her to make decisions even against the opinion of Chardonnet, who left law school to join the maquis, received his political education from a friend during the war, and became federal secretary without ever having been a worker. But he has learned the technique of command. During the evening planning the demonstration and the strike: "Chardonnet laissa les coudes franches à Pierrette. Il n'était certainement pas venu dans cette intention. Mais Pierrette s'imposait à nous tous . . ." (369).

There are many pressures and forces, both individual and societal, working against Pierrette and her position as militant leader. First, there is her own biological nature. Climbing through the woods behind Beau Masque: "Son sang battit plus chaud dans son ventre. Elle fut furieuse contre elle-même. . . . Il y avait des mois et des mois qu'elle n'avait pas éprouvé cela" (157). She also needs to be comforted: "Elle eut envie de se serrer contre lui et de sangloter tout à son aise dans le creux de son bras" (201). It is neither of these reasons which causes her to set up housekeeping with him, but rather the personal and political necessity of proving to Émilie that she is wrong. In her case, as with Marat during the war, the personal and the political are the same thing since it is from the political activity and her ability to continue it successfully that she gains her self-respect.

But self-respect is not human warmth. She begins to fall into the trap of domesticity, which is made more attractive by the reactions of others in the community. Before her liaison with Beau Masque she rarely saw her friend Marguerite, who "avait approuvé en gros l'action de Pierrette, mais elle n'avait plus eu envie de se raconter à une amie qui avait renoncé à toute vie privée." (287). Marguerite talks to her more frequently after she begins living with Beau Masque, and Pierrette thinks she has many comrades all over the world: "Mais elle n'avait qu'une amie, et c'était Marguerite. Il était doux d'avoir aussi une amie" (334). In her solitude she was looked upon by the others as "une étrangère": "On n'avait pas eu un mot de blâme pour elle; on avait admis, sans même avoir besoin d'en parler, qu'elle défendait les intérêts de tous, mais qu'elle y consacrât toute sa vie avait paru inexplicable" (287). They continued to vote for her, but they no longer thought of her or called upon her as a woman in times of domestic crisis or joy. After she begins living with Beau Masque, however, they all find little ways of expressing their approval that she has once again become "une femme." To some men, however, her being a woman like any other woman means that she is fair game, as seen in Jean's rape attempt.

The physical changes accompanying her pregnancy present another kind of danger for her calling as "une révolutionnaire professionnelle": "Elle se sentait sans défense, comme une sentinelle qui s'est laissé arracher son arme par surprise" (294). She remembers that for most of the women she knows: "La maternité avait été un malheur, le commencement de la résignation, un point final à la lutte," and she herself "était trop lasse pour replacer, comme elle le faisait d'habitude, l'événement qui la concernait si intimement dans la perspective du socialisme" (294). After the period of sickness and nightmares passes, she feels much better, "et elle était heureuse de s'endormir contre le corps musculeux, femme parmi les autres femmes" (297).

In Pierrette's "professional" life there are other trials and temptations, doubts about the efficacy of the work in Le Clusot, dreams of leaving for the cities "où les grands militants se trempent dans le bruit des forges, des laminoirs et des marteaux-pilons" (318), the "sourire complice" of members of higher echelons of management inviting her to play their game because they respect her, have confidence in her, and judge her "à sa juste valeur" as "un adversaire d'égale finesse" (323). One of her main trials is her impatience with other workers, especially "combinards," who have another job or a farm in order to live better, but then have no time to enjoy this better life. She also is not certain she has the patience to work until the "revolution" and its aftermath. She is so listless because of her pregnancy and because of the lack of excitement about the demonstration that she cannot even get upset when Marguerite decides to work in the new project to receive higher wages:

> Elle n'avait même pas de chagrin. Elle sentait seulement encore un peu plus lasse que la veille et l'avant-veille et tous ces jours consacrés à un combat dont l'issue lui parut soudain si lointaine, dont elle sentit soudain dans son corps que l'issue était encore immensément lointaine, qu'elle trébucha. (335-36)

However, the firing of the workers, ordered by Valerio Empoli, unites the workers, and they all look to Pierrette. She is president of the strike committee, where all the unions are represented. Mignot thinks she acted too quickly without consulting anyone in the Party hierarchy outside Le Clusot, but she realizes that a delay of one day would have been disastrous:

> Maintenant que les piquets de grève sont à leur poste, même les lâches n'oseront pas revenir sur la décision prise à l'unanimité; nous avons crée une situation où il faut plus de courage pour se dégonfler devant les ouvriers que devant les patrons; même la lâcheté travaille aujourd'hui pour nous. (355)

The novel is a means of perhaps recruiting others to help Pierrette. It at least reveals a situation in all its complexity showing how workers can let themselves be taken in by, acted upon by, the forces of management and showing that Pierrette's way could lead to a better life for all. It also shows how an individual can be trapped by a value-system without being aware of it. The outlook of the novel is optimistic, based on the idea that each person has a place, an assigned role in life, which he must learn to play, rather than try to escape, and based also on a recognition of human worth and respect for the good qualities in all.

Throwing heroism out entirely in favor of a plodding daily battle is, however, too extreme a position. Could even Pierrette do this for the rest of her life, especially if Valerio Empoli were not around to save the day? What if the most exciting thing that ever happened was the annual bicycle race? 325.000 francs is a picture of a town not far from Le Clusot where the situation is different and where the position of the writer reflects this difference. Bionnas is described as an animated industrial city which the writer likes to visit late in the afternoon amid the noise of the motor scooters, the shops full of women, and the brilliance of the shopwindows. This brilliance and animation are revealing and deceptive, and the novel focuses on a small number of characters moving in an extremely limited world with a limited, almost primitive view of that world, characters who are, like the oak trees in La Grange-aux-Vents, "pourris du coeur." Everything in Bionnas is seen as artificial and empty, the life is based on competition and exploitation with very little hope of change because the characters on whom the novel focuses are, in general, selfish, interested in narrowly personal goals, and certainly not capable of living on "the cutting edge of history" as Pierrette was. The difference is immediately seen in the titles of the two novels, one the name of a man, the other a sum of money.

Bionnas is "le principal centre français de production d'objets en matière plastique" (5), and, unlike Le Clusot, which had remained virtually unchanged in size for many years, it has grown tremendously since the birth of the plastics industry and the invention of injection presses about 1936. Most of the industrialists in Bionnas are former artisans made rich by the presses. Jules Morel, owner of Plastoform and of the low-cost, low-quality housing complex where Marie-Jeanne and her mother live and of other real estate from which he hopes to make money when his competitors want to expand, came to Bionnas thirty years previously as a day laborer, saw the injection presses near his wife's home in Germany, and realized that he had discovered "l'arme qui lui permettra de conquérir Bionnas" (83), which he proceeded to do. / His son Paul grew up in Bionnas, went to grammar school with young men who are now his workers, whom he calls "tu" and from whom he borrows money, his father not trusting him with enough for his tastes. Like Philippe in Beau Masque, he insists that he knows nothing at all about the business, which will probably collapse when he takes over.

Job opportunities in the industries in Bionnas are limited to two categories: "les mécaniciens qui fabriquent les moules . . . un métier de haute précision" (68), requiring a long apprenticeship; and the manual workers who run the presses, for whom no advancement is possible:

> L'homme qui a commencé à travailler à la presse ne quittera plus jamais la presse. Faute de pouvoir augmenter le salaire horaire, il travaillera davantage d'heures. Il commencera par huit heures par jour à l'usine. Puis, pour pouvoir acheter une cuisinière à gaz ou un scooter, il fera des heures supplémentaires chez les artisans qui achètent d'occasion les vieilles presses à injecter. Il travaillera toujours plus longtemps; il mangera et dormira pour pouvoir travailler; et rien d'autre jusqu'à la mort. (68)

It is work requiring no training, no skill, and work which can be done the first day as well as it can be done after fifty years. The men who "serve" the presses are seen as machines or as animals, but never as men. The only reason they are used instead of fully automatic machines is that they are cheaper. In the factories women do the work of assembling and finishing products made by the presses. Outside the factories there are former artisans who finish products not completed in the factories.

Bernard Busard, twenty-two years old, is already too old to begin the training and apprenticeship necessary to become a mechanic. Unlike Lamballe and Beau-Masque, who were also hemmed in by their pasts, Busard is seen to be short-sighted because anyone growing up in Bionnas is aware of the conditions. In the beginning of the novel, however, he does not work in the factories; his "métier" is riding a tricycle carrying mass-produced plastic objects from the factories to the workers who finish them. His ambition is to leave Bionnas, preferably to undertake a career in bicycle racing, for which purpose he has bought a racing bicycle and practices every day after work. He is courting Marie-Jeanne Lemercier, who also does not work in the factory, but makes handmade lingerie at home.

The novel opens the first Sunday in May 1954, with the annual bicycle race, which turns out to be a battle between Busard and Le Bressan, a young man from the country, who has tremendous animal strength but no technique. Busard leaves the rest of the cyclists behind and takes out in pursuit of Le Bressan, who wins the race, while Busard, beset by accidents, comes in fourth. On the Tuesday after the race, Marie-Jeanne promises to marry Busard when he finds a "vrai métier" and a house. She specifies that she means a job not connected with plastics and not in Bionnas. Busard leaves town and comes back with an option to buy the franchise on a snack bar on the highway between Paris and Nice if he can raise 700,000 francs. The savings of his family and of Marie-Jeanne's amount to 375,000 francs, which means that he must find some way of raising 325,000 francs. Although union rules forbid working at the presses more than eight hours a day, he manages to get himself and Le Bressan hired to "serve" one press, working in four-hour shifts. Thus the aim is to work twelve hours a day for one hundred and eighty-seven days to earn 325,000 francs, the snack bar, and Marie-Jeanne. Le Bressan will also earn the same amount, and there will be enough left over to pay room and board to Busard's parents; he and Le Bressan share a room because they are never there at the same time.

Toward the end of the ordeal, the company installs new machines which operate faster, for which the union negotiates an increase in the hourly wage. During the break while the machines are being installed, Busard and Le Bressan go cycling together and get acquainted. Although the wage increase means that Busard will earn his 325,000 francs two shifts earlier than planned, he has his calendar all set up with the days marked off and intends to work the planned number of shifts. On the last day, Busard becomes so hypnotized by the machine that his arm is caught in the press and has to be amputated. While he is delirious in the hospital, Marie-Jeanne takes the 325,000 francs to the snack bar owner, who refuses to sell because the clientele would not like being served by a one-armed man, who could not do the work anyway; he does, however, return the 375,000 francs paid originally. Jambe d'Argent, who runs a local bar with an unsavory reputation lets it be known that he will sell his bar for two million francs, of which 800,000 is to be in cash. He at first refuses to lower the price to 700,000, which is the amount Marie-Jeanne has, but he suddenly changes his mind and sells the bar to Busard and Marie-Jeanne for 700,000 francs plus one million to be paid on time, thus lowering the price by 300,000 francs. Busard, who knows that Jambe d'Argent would never let this amount of money go, is suspicious of Marie-Jeanne, thinking she sold her favors to old man Morel to get the money. His suspicions and his bad temper drive customers away, and they soon lose the bar. They move in with Marie-Jeanne's mother, and both of them go to work for Plastoform; Busard will make ten francs an hour more than before because a strike called in protest over his accident won this increase for the workers. It turns out that Le Bressan had given the 300,000 francs, but had sworn Jambe d'Argent to secrecy because he was ashamed of his gift, thinking people would make fun of him.

The characters in _Beau Masque_ were in the end able to assess themselves and their position and to judge themselves; in _325.000 francs_ it is the author as a character in the novel who judges them, according to a system of values which is obviously different from theirs, and it is his presence as moral judge which represents any optimism which is to be found in the novel. He lives on the side of a mountain and is married; although he talks to the other characters and is invited to their homes, most of his discussions are held with his wife. All his dealings with the other characters are on a personal basis; there is no "comradeship" and no great work of changing the face of the earth. He makes clear that he and his wife discuss their acquaintances and judge them:

> Cordélia et moi, nous avons l'habitude de faire l'épreuve de l'intégrité des syndicalistes, des hommes d'affaires, des politiciens et des jeunes femmes, en confrontant, aussi impitoyablement qu'un contrôleur des contributions, leur train de vie et leurs gains avoués. (135-36)

Throughout the novel he gives his personal reactions to the characters and events. Speaking of Busard's treatment of Chatelard, the union secretary, he writes: "Je fus agacé qu'il eût floué le vieux délégué, dont j'avais eu l'occasion d'apprécier l'intelligence claire et la fermeté d'âme" (124). He expresses his opinion of Busard and of Marie-Jeanne:

> Toute cette affaire est absurde. Marie-Jeanne est sèche; comment peut-on aimer une femme qui pince les lèvres comme elle fait? Busard est un maladroit de l'avoir poursuivie

> pendant dix-huit mois, sans l'obtenir. Il me plaisait tant qu'il voulait gagner le Tour de France. Maintenant qu'il fait des bassesses pour devenir boutiquier, il me dégoûte. (125)

The bicycle race which opens the book is, like the hunt which opens Les Mauvais Coups, a paradigm of life and of the book. It is a competitive event in which there are winners and losers; it has a commercial aspect in that monetary prizes are given by businesses for winning and also for winning different stages of the race. Early winners may not be the final winner, and some will win nothing at all. The event is composed of the racers; their trainers and managers; the spectators who, like the author, follow the race in cars, shout encouragement or advice to the racers and have a broader perspective than the competitors themselves because of their greater mobility; and the spectators who remain in one spot watching the race as it goes by. Even these spectators have an influence on the race; it is a child from one of these stationary groups who, trying to get a better view, causes Busard's accident.

This race brings together "les meilleurs amateurs de six départements" (6), those who have already proved that they are better than the average amateur. But all the racers, with the exception of Le Bressan, belong to clubs, wear the colors of their club, and in general follow the tactics worked out by their managers: "Le cerveau, voilà avec quoi on gagne les courses" (12). Within each club there is one racer who has proved himself to be the best, and the strategy of the club is built around him and what he can be expected to do. The general tactic of all the experienced racers is to remain with the group as long as possible so as not to tire too easily, and in any case to pace themselves with another racer. In a grueling race like this one it is the final sprint which determines the winner because at this point "on se bat davantage avec le coeur (Rodrigue as-tu du coeur?) qu'avec le muscle ou le souffle" (15). The author comments: "les amateurs, dans ces courses de province, mènent souvent plus rudement que les professionnels des grandes épreuves, qui s'entendent tacitement pour ménager leurs forces" (15).

The existence and identity of Le Bressan are so much a part of his land and his region that he has no other name in the novel; the customs of his people are presented in the same light as those of "les indigènes de la Nouvelle-Guinée" (73). He is an amateur among amateurs; in fact, he is not really an amateur, he is "hors série," so to speak. This is his "année de conscrit," the year preceding his military service, during which, according to custom, he is to devote himself to daring exploits. He decides to devote his year to "des prouesses sportives" and takes up cycling because the prize money in the races during the summer will permit him to "tenir table ouverte à l'auberge. Il sera doublement champion de cyclisme et de générosité" (76). This year of prowess thus constitutes a kind of rite of passage into manhood, a year which has no relation to the rest of his life except it will furnish the image of himself which he will carry for the rest of his life, a life which has already been planned and which follows the pattern of his father's life "et rien d'autre jusqu'à la mort" (76).

He buys an old bicycle, not a racer, and teaches and trains himself. He does not even understand the principle of the gears and certainly not the tactics of the group; on the one afternoon when he and Busard go riding together, however, he catches on quickly to the techniques taught by Busard. But he wins the opening race without these techniques; he is described as an animal with no style, and the author says he has "du coeur" like "un boeuf de labour" (37). He wins the race and others during the summer despite the author's contention that: "Ce sont toujours les plus forts qui gagnent, les plus rusés, ceux qui ont le plus d'expérience, les plus intelligents, ceux qui savent triompher de leur nature" (41). The others, despite their complicated machines and their tactics, are simply not as strong as he is, especially because he is giving his all without reserving anything for another season. He is obviously a savage and perhaps not a noble savage, but he is attempting to prove his worth. This proof, however, will in no way actually affect his life later, and he does not really understand why he is doing it; it is simply custom. His gift to Busard and Marie-Jeanne and his attitude toward it represent a mixture of old values of nobility with newer materialistic values, but he is not intelligent enough to unmix them and is too superstitious to try.

The next step up the ladder of heroism is the medieval knight who performs feats of valor to prove himself worthy of the fair lady. Marie-Jeanne lives with her mother, a worker at Plastoform, where Marie-Jeanne has stubbornly refused to join her. She makes fine handmade underclothes for the wives of the nouveaux riches, who think this is a sign of quality. She sits, framed by the window and in view of passersby, sewing all day and permits Busard to visit her at specifically authorized times following a strict ritual schedule. Marie-Jeanne is contrasted with another young woman in town, Juliette, who is open and spontaneous, while Marie-Jeanne is the opposite. Her mother says of her that she has never known what she wanted: "Elle a surtout appris à savoir ce qu'elle ne voulait pas" (120). While Juliette wears her hair long so it flies in the breeze when she rides her scooter, Marie-Jeanne is always perfectly groomed without a hair out of place. The regular undulations of her hair are "comme les tuiles d'un toit qui vient d'être achevé"; her eyes are "comme des volets fraîchement peints" (56):

> Des yeux du bleu qu'on dit d'émail, qui accrochent la lumière et qui renvoient, mais qui n'ont ni profondeur, ni vivacité. . . . C'était comme si Marie-Jeanne avait posé de petites cuirasses sur ses prunelles. Les yeux de Marie-Jeanne: une aile de coléoptère dans chaque orbite, un coléoptère lisse, net, brillant, poli, un coléoptère de joaillerie, soigneusement poncé. (138-39)

Her forehead is "bombé, lustré comme les rondes bosses des vieilles argenteries" (139). She has "une singulière unité de style" and a pleasant laugh, "mais pas un de ces rires éclatants, explosion de vie, qui me donnent envie de vivre encore mille ans" (140). It is obvious that Marie-Jeanne has made of herself a fortress in which she feels safe, but she has thus made of herself an object different from others.

The author recognizes that Juliette is temporarily free because she has not yet been humiliated. In the end of the novel she leaves Bionnas with a traveling salesman and spends her time in bars in Lyons, having already lost "l'éclat qui faisait penser à une montagne au printemps" (238). Marie-Jeanne's façade is a defense against further humiliation after having experienced a pregnancy and a painful abortion, but the defense acts as a lure. This lure is at least partly conscious; she takes pleasure in torturing the old men who are attracted to her: "L'esclave croit éternelle la triste sagesse que lui ont enseignée des siècles de cohabitation avec le maître" (52). This process is expressed, as in _Les Mauvais Coups_, in terms of the hare and the hounds and the master and the slave, illustrated by the colonial master and the "boy," every woman being in relation to every man "un Nègre." The author contends that Marie-Jeanne is playing the master, but that the roles would be reversed "dans l'instant même où leur désir éveillerait un écho chez elle" (132).

This is what happens on the Tuesday after the race, but Busard is so busy telling her how much he loves her, how much he has sacrificed for her, and how much he is willing to sacrifice, that the moment passes without his taking advantage of his opportunity. Realizing the danger, she tries to back out of her promise to marry him. But the pressure of having everyone she knows, including the author's wife, tell her that she owes it to him because he loves her so much, has courted her so assiduously and so faithfully, is more than she can withstand. Later, on the one occasion she comes to the factory while he is working, she is so moved by his weak, sweating body sacrificing so much for her that she is caught both by the sacrifice and by the maternal wish to take care of him: "'Je suis heureuse,' dit-elle, avec élan. Hélène fut surprise, ayant toujours connu Marie-Jeanne parfaitement maîtresse d'elle-même" (221). The loss of his arm permanently binds her to him in a circular creditor-debtor relationship.

Busard, who has large eyes "sans secret" (60), and who repeats throughout the novel: "Je veux vivre aujourd'hui" (110) and "J'ai envie de faire tout ce qui me plaît" (164), is obviously a child. Marie-Jeanne sees him and Le Bressan as "des enfants qui lancent leurs billes sur un jeu de boules où des adultes sont en train de calculer leurs coups" (59). In contrast to Le Bressan, he has the intelligence to try to get out of what is obviously a hopeless situation, but he does not really understand what makes it hopeless and ends up even more entangled in the system of exploitation and materialistic values. He wants to become a professional racer because he will have time to practice and will make progress, but he will also be a hero: "Il n'est pas homme à faire toute sa carrière comme 'domestique' des géants de la route. Il saura dire: voilà mes conditions, c'est à prendre ou à laisser; et au besoin s'échapper du peloton contre la volonté du directeur d'équipe" (58). What he really wants are visible symbols of his success, "une Cadillac décapotable, carrosserie sport, pas de sièges arrière" (58), and Marie-Jeanne, who is "précieuse," a luxury item. Once he has decided that he wants her, he is, as the author specifies, enchained by "le mécanisme de la passion" (142). He is not aware of his reasons for choosing her and does not begin to have intimations of what he has lost until it is too late. During a break from his work with the press he admits to the author that Marie-Jeanne is not very affectionate and says to Juliette:

"Tu as du coeur. . . . Tu es bien plus belle que Marie-Jeanne. Tu es meilleure qu'elle. Je me sens mieux avec toi. Pourquoi est-ce que j'aime Marie-Jeanne?" (176).

Throughout the opening race Busard shouts to Marie-Jeanne: "C'est pour vous" (44), and on the Tuesday after the race he tells her that: "Tout ce qu'il attendait de la vie, c'était qu'elle l'autorisât de dormir chaque nuit près d'elle et de lui apporter chaque semaine son salaire. Pour l'amour d'elle et si elle l'exigeait, il renoncera même à la carrière de coureur" (62-63). He, the entire town, and eventually Marie-Jeanne romanticize his work and see it as the trial of a knight to win the hand of the lady, even though the feat is to get the money to buy her using any means. The author calls this "le ton de l'époque," which is characterized by a lack of grandeur and heroism "comme dans Corneille" (125), showing that he also has his heroic models he would like to be able to follow. One of the means Busard uses is lying; he lies to Chatelard, telling him that Marie-Jeanne is pregnant, even though lying does not yet come "naturally" to him. While telling the lie: "Il s'appuyait d'une jambe sur l'autre. Il regardait la bouche du vieil homme, pour ne pas avoir l'air de fuir son regard, mais quand même ne pas rencontrer ses yeux" (109).

The snack bar for which he makes great plans is a structure made of concrete blocks with six gas pumps and a neon sign which remains lit all night. He plans to offer curb service: "S'ils ne veulent pas quitter leur siège, on leur porte un sandwich, avec du vin dans un goblet de carton" (72). He plans in ten years to be able to buy the place with their savings, add more employees, and perhaps buy a chain of snack bars between Paris and Nice, each with no name, but with a number corresponding to the number of miles the travelers have come or still have to go. Busard's father works at home with his wife and daughter polishing frames for plastic eyeglasses and has the illusion of being his own boss because he can go fishing whenever he pleases. Since they contract to do a certain amount of work in a certain amount of time, the women have to do their work and his while he fishes. However, he and Chatelard both disapprove of the snack bar, saying that Busard only wants to exploit people, and Jules Morel talks to him as to a fellow capitalist. Neither Busard's father nor Chatelard has anything better to suggest than to do the work they do, although Chatelard says: "À ton âge, je rêvais de faire la révolution, de libérer tous les travailleurs. Je n'ai pas changé d'ailleurs. Lutter pour que tout le monde ait droit 'au pain et aux roses,' ça ne te dit rien à toi?" (109). One sign of hope is his statement that he may not really know young people, but that it seems to him there are some who are "faits d'une bonne matière" (112). Neither Busard's father nor Chatelard makes any real objection to the exploit or to the marriage. Chatelard, "qui prépare une grève en faisant l'analyse du marché" (109), who is the leader of the local union (obviously F. O.), and who can explain to the union delegate from Paris exactly how the workers are being exploited, abstains from deciding whether Busard and Le Bressan should be allowed to work twelve hours a day. He leaves the decision to the other delegates because: "Je ne peux pas être impartial, parce que j'aime bien la Marie-Jeanne, et ça ne me plaît pas qu'elle se marie avec un petit gars qui se conduit mal" (112). The other delegates, "moins rigoureux que Chatelard sur les principes" (112), present no opposition.

Busard at the beginning of the race exults because he is "en pleine forme," which contrasts with the "forme en creux" which he makes at the press and with the somnambulant state in which he makes it. Obviously the "form" needed for cycling is not the "form" needed for working at the press. His passion for Marie-Jeanne and the resulting passion to complete the task cause him to set a goal which taxes him beyond his powers. He chooses to make the money doing something which he has not been trained to do, in the sense that he has no experience with the work and no real conception of how it will affect him. Like a racer obsessed by the "délai d'arrivée," he looks upon the time spent at the press as "un temps mort," taking away from his time for living. Trying to shorten this "temps mort," he calculates without allowing himself a margin of safety. The desire to escape, when it becomes a passion, is just like any other passion and is, in the eyes of the author, self-defeating and enslaving. As with Beau Masque, accepting this "temps mort" even temporarily has disastrous results.

The derisory nature of the envisioned future compares with that of the end product of the work and the means to manufacture that product. The characters old Letourneau, Aimé Amable, and Émilie Empoli illustrated this fact in _Beau Masque_. In _325.000 francs_ the machine in which all the characters are caught is a second-hand technological marvel bought from an American company. The product is a plastic toy, or rather "le bas-relief de deux carrosses symétriques posés l'un sur l'autre" (97). In another part of the factory, women lined up at a table finish the toy, each woman doing one operation all day long. The machine and its product, in addition to ridiculing the division of labor and the complicated process to achieve such a derisory result, form a metaphor for life, as evidenced by the sexual nature of the machine: "Le va-et-vient du piston, le long cylindre dardé au creux du ventre et l'injection de la matière plastique en fusion dans la matrice du moule, font l'objet, parmi les travailleurs de la matière plastique, d'innombrables plaisanteries" (94).

The life of each individual can thus be seen as a result of the materials used, the mold into which this material is pressed, the processes and influences it undergoes until it is finished, and the use made of it after its completion. The same would hold true for the life, or history, of mankind. This particular machine, the American capitalist machine based on exploitation and possession, makes a plastic product, like Busard, who is not made of good material; which is hollow, like Marie-Jeanne, who is all façade; and which is subjected to an over-powering number of influences, like Le Bressan, who is strong, solid, and generous, but burdened with custom, superstition, and ignorance. The product is a toy Louis XIV carriage sold in Africa; in America the same machine made the same object, but in black, and it was used as publicity for a funeral home. Both uses are seen as exploitation of the weak by the strong, with also perhaps the idea that a life lived in accordance with a certain view of "nobility" is the way of death.

The work at the machine, like the product itselt, is seen as an empty shell, a series of gestures to be made interminably, gestures having no significance beyond themselves, although Le Bressan sees them as magic gestures because he is rewarded with money. His work is compared to religious processions in his home town praying for rain in dry seasons, a kind of primitive rain dance. This is not work, in his opinion, because no effort is required. But he, like Busard, soon discovers the deadening effect of the monotony of the work, the strain on the entire body leading to the somnambulant state in which Busard keeps telling himself he must stop to cut on the current to the safety grill, envisages his hand being caught in the machine, and is so hypnotized by this thought that it actually happens.

This work of empty gestures is contrasted with writing and cycling or the work of anyone "pour qui l'exécution d'un travail est une création toujours nouvelle et dont l'issue n'est jamais sûre" (34). This kind of work requires that the person be "en forme," which the author defines as being "dans les règles pour gagner" (32). He defines form as "l'extrême pointe de l'éveil" (118):

> La forme s'oppose à la matière, au sens où l'athlète sent la matière comme un poids qui freine la performance: pour que l'athlète soit en forme, il faut que la graisse, la lymphe, tout ce qui alourdit, se soit transformé en nerfs et en muscles, que la matière soit devenue forme. L'athlète parfait s'imagine flamme se consumant dans la performance sans laisser de cendres. (32)

During the race at the beginning of the novel, the author is an amateur of cycling in that he is an informed spectator, one who knows the rules and understands what the race is about and what conditions are necessary to win. This is also the kind of spectator of life he shows himself to be during the course of the novel. But what he really enjoys about the race is getting into the spirit of the event, experiencing vicariously what the racers themselves are experiencing, watching their faces and trying to compare what they must be feeling with what he has felt, sharing their feeling but also envying it: "J'imaginais l'exaltation de Busard et je l'enviais" (28). He thinks Busard must be feeling "la même allégresse que lorsque je viens d'achever un chapitre dont je suis content" (33). He says that he feels for athletes a kind of "fraternelle tendresse" because, according to him, for the writer who has attained "maturity" and who has something to say, "la forme" becomes his primary preoccupation because he has solved his own interior conflicts. His problems are now those of humanity: "Ainsi tend-il à retrouver l'innocence du sportif qui ne pense qu'à sa forme, qui ne parle que d'elle et qui, à l'approche des grandes épreuves s'impose pour l'amour d'elle, sobriété et chasteté" (33).

Busard does not realize until he has already given it up what it really meant to be a member of "la cohorte des héros qui renoncent volontairement aux petites facilités. . . . Il n'aurait jamais plus rien à sacrifier à la forme" (117). It is obvious that, despite emphasis on what organization of the workers might be able to achieve in improved working conditions and higher wages, the author feels that Busard was right in trying to escape; the fact is, the work is simply not worth doing, but neither is the work at the snack bar. Busard's only chance to live with any semblance of freedom and dignity was to remain with his original plan to try to become a professional cyclist. Ideals of heroism inherited from earlier societies are not the same when placed in the context of present-day society; cycling, if approached and practiced for the right reasons, can lead to heroism, professional heroism on a continuing basis. The performance itself can be bought and sold, but "la forme" remains an individual conquest.

The author, however, is not actually a hero when he writes. He makes clear that in a real race, there comes a point beyond being "en forme," when "le coeur" takes over. During the race he has to use memories of war or passion at that time to feel what Busard is feeling because it is not a part of writing. But in his writing the author is "en forme," that is he makes sacrifices in order to achieve this highest state of wakefulness necessary to perform, and he does it as a professional on a continuing basis. He can do this even if there are no strikes or demonstrations and even if there are no bicycle races. He can write a novel about working overtime and about the complex system of values and assumptions associated with it. He can still feel a fraternal link with the characters even though they are not, as in Beau Masque, actually participating together in the same concrete action; he can find in their experiences analogies to his own experience because he is, after all, living in the same society and subject to the same influences.

THE WORLD

La Loi, written after the revelations of the Twentieth Party Congress and the beginning of the process of de-stalinization, was published in 1957. It is a fictional world left to its own devices, so to speak; it is the same kind of world *325.000 francs* would have been if the author had not been present. The novel is a description of Porto Manacore, a town on the Adriatic coast of southern Italy, where the only writers are amateur scholars who write of times long dead, and even the newspapers have little impact. It is the kind of "creux" described by Marat in *Drôle de Jeu*, a physical and moral vacuum untouched by the winds of change:

> Mais jamais la moindre brise n'a effleuré Manacore, comme si les combattants du large avaient aspiré tout l'air de la baie, comme si tout l'espace entre les hautes crêtes rocheuses et le large formait un creux dans l'atmosphère, une poche vide d'air, l'intérieur d'une ventouse. (40)

The unchanging monotony is exemplified by the lack of any divisions in the text itself, with only double spacing to show a shift in focus. Obvious echoes of previous novelistic worlds, especially those of Marivaux, Balzac, Stendhal, and Flaubert, are used differently from such echoes in previous novels of Vailland, where they showed his lucid recognition that he was using them to his own purposes and was not being acted upon by them unconsciously. This same element is present here with the additional emphasis on the fact that the society which the earlier novelists portrayed still exists; society has not changed and the new man has not appeared.

The novel makes clear that the problems of exploitation and possessiveness do not come only from the capitalistic system, but from the idea of hierarchy itself, as best seen in the organization of the Catholic church. Porto Manacore is a feudal society based on an agrarian economy, a society stratified in a rigid hierarchy, where there are many goats, but no unicorns or heroes because they are not possible within the limited possibilities of the closed system. Matteo Brigante, the gangster who controls Porto Manacore, sees the world in the image of the royal navy when he was a quartermaster: sailors at the bottom and God at the top (230). When he was younger he had a simpler idea of the hierarchy, but with the same top and bottom:

> Don Ottavio faisait attendre son métayer qui faisait attendre son ouvrier agricole. Le Roi faisait probablement attendre don Ottavio et Dieu le Roi. . . . Chacun attend quelqu'un et fait attendre quelqu'un d'autre. Seul Dieu n'attend personne et seul l'ouvrier agricole n'a personne à faire attendre. (242)

The town is built in just this same way beginning at sea level with the poor people in the Vieille Ville and ending with the Sanctuary of Saint Ursula of Uria at the top, "les maisons juxtaposées et enchevêtrées les unes aux autres, les unes dans les autres, la terrasse de celle-ci formant la cour de celle-là, chaque chambre, grenier ou cave d'une autre chambre, depuis le môle du port jusqu'au sanctuaire de sainte Ursule d'Uria" (63). The artificiality of the stratification and the minimal differences between the standards of living of the different classes in Porto Manacore is seen by the division of the public beach:

> Une toute petite plage, tirée d'un trait, du môle du port jusqu'à l'orangerie de don Ottavio. Du large, on ne la distingue pas des murs de soutènement des jardins d'orangers et de citronniers qui touchent à la route. Trois sociétés cependant s'y côtoient, avec chacune son territoire précisément délimité, bien que nulle barricade ni ligne d'aucune sorte n'en marquent les frontières. (212)

History is also seen as a series of stratifications, the piling up of layer upon layer with no progress, or as a process of "the eternal return," but with a downward rather than upward spiral, like the Maelstrom image in <u>Drôle de</u>

Jeu. All the public buildings of the town are hundreds of years old, reflecting the history of the town, but the people who inhabit these buildings either know nothing of that history or make no connections between history and their lives. The wooden statue of Venus dredged up from the swamp becomes, draped in clothing "à l'espagnole," the statue of Saint Ursula, devoted to the cult of virginity.

Porto Manacore is a town where everyone is either a prisoner or unemployed (_désoccupé_) or both. The prisoners in the town jail are placed in the center of town on the main square, aware of everything that is going on, subjected all day to radio broadcasts over the loudspeaker. In _Drôle de Jeu_ the radio was described as "le mécanisme compliqué qui donnait corps à toutes les voix du monde" (237), but in Porto Manacore the radio plays popular music with words in French. The prisoners do not understand the words and give their own interpretations to the music, just as the inhabitants, who do not understand anything that is happening in the world at present or anything in their past history, formulate individual philosophies of life and of history, if they think about them at all. All the voices of the world in _Drôle de Jeu_ have become _la voix_, a natural gift associated with sorcery. The ever-present _désoccupés_, described as _méduses_, convey the petrification of the individual and of society and at the same time the jellyfish consistency of the moral fiber.

It is a society where, in the words of Attilio, the police commissioner: "Tout le monde est le flic de tout le monde. Les autres font par plaisir ce que je fais par métier" (67). It is a society where even in the mosquito-infested swamp there are ever-vigilant eyes:

> La plage est sous l'oeil de la route, les jardins sous les yeux des autres jardins et les olivaies sous les yeux de tout le monde. Les forestiers . . . parcourent à cheval la forêt. . . . Les collines sont sous l'oeil des gardiens de chèvres,

> le marais sous l'oeil des pêcheurs et les barques qui prennent la mer sous tous les yeux de la côte. (178)

Seeing, which in Drôle de Jeu and in Les Mauvais Coups was synonymous with lucidity and understanding, has become a means of entrapment, and light has become the "soleil-lion," which dazzles the sight and induces torpor. The trabucco, the only technical invention in the book represented as having any beneficial use for mankind, is perhaps one or two thousand years old and is a mechanism for trapping fish and closing the trap by raising the net at the right time, "une pêche à vue" (194). The trabucco itself represents a lack of technical progress and, by its juxtaposition to the meeting of Lucrezia and Francesco in the cave, a lack of progress in human relations and particularly in relations between men and women:

> Chaque année, le trabucco se renouvelle un peu. Après les grandes tempêtes, les pêcheurs remplacent un mât, changent un câble. Mais ni la technique ni la forme changent. Chaque année différent et toujours le même, le trabucco est là depuis des centaines et sans doute des milliers d'années. (195)

As was the case with Beau Masque, the novel is primarily a description of a system, its effect on individual lives, and the relative success or failure of individual responses to the system; the system is the same which Beau Masque, once he had "seen" it, refused. La Loi is Vailland's definitive lucid examination and repudiation of the "homme à femmes" in the tradition of Don Juan, his definitive recognition of the lack of freedom implied by negations, and his recognition of Sade's discovery of the impossibility of "liberté et égalité." The main plot mechanism is the theft two weeks before the opening of the novel of 500,000 lire from a Swiss couple camping in the area. The events in the novel take place within a period of seventy-two hours, but each character is seen in relation to his past, and the end of the novel reveals what happened to each one in the next few years and what the future can be expected to bring. The real plot is the process by which everyone is master to someone and slave to someone else in a vicious cycle of domination and humiliation.

Success in this society involves having as many eyes as possible, like Matteo and Attilio and their informers or like Pippo and his second in command in the street gang: "Pippo regardait Matteo Brigante, Balbo surveillait la place. Quand ils sont ensemble, c'est comme une seule tête qui tient les quatre points cardinaux dans un seul regard" (118). Everyone is aware that he is playing to an audience which understands the game or the play: "Devant un public aussi averti de toutes les nuances de la vie sociale, Giuseppina joue à jeu découvert. Elle le sait aussi bien que son public" (234). The code of honor is based, not on a personal feeling of worth or of humiliation, but on public display. After don Cesare and others like him have taken advantage of their "droits de seigneur," the families fabricate a false virginity for the girls. The same conception of honor is seen in the behavior of don Cesare with his relatives in the days before he lost interest in the world. The relatives all hoped to inherit something from don Cesare, who tried to goad them into exhibiting some spark of self-respect, which is a part of his own code of honor and is, like himself, a relic of a dead past. One of the ways he tried to do this was by fondling the young girls in front of their parents, who simply moved to the other end of the room and pretended to be deep in conversation so that "leur honneur" would not cause them to intervene. The girls themselves would not have minded if he had done the same thing in private, having been brought up to see this as their lot in life, but they knew it was a deliberate offense to do it in public.

Matteo Brigante understands this code of honor and accepts it. While he was in the navy he waited two years until the right set of circumstances allowed him to get revenge without counter revenge for verbal insults about his mother and mistress delivered "devant tout l'équipage aligné sur le pont" (269). When Mariette marks his face with his own knife, he makes up a story that a virgin marked him while he was raping her, which is perfectly all right: "Sang pour sang, il n'y a pas offense" (270). He is relieved to find out from the pharmacist that cosmetic surgery will be able to erase the marks, and so he goes home "doublement allégé quant à la marque par le _sangue_ _per_ _sangue_ du serveur du bar et par la promesse du pharmacien" (281). Private humiliation is not seen as humiliation; it is the public "exécution" which counts, as in Attilio's letting Giuseppina make him appear ridiculous in front of the assembled public on the beach. Matteo keeps up his front; soon after returning home from his defeat and marking at the hands of Mariette, he brags to Giuseppina: "La fille qui défendra quelque chose à Matteo Brigante n'est pas encore née" (286). The artificiality of his façade and of hers is emphasized by his trying to pinch her breasts and feeling only "l'armature du soutien-gorge" (288).

The best defense in this society is a façade of impassivity like that of Marie-Jeanne in _325.000_ _francs_. Matteo has spent his life amassing a fortune and training his son as a weopon to use against businessmen who will try to take this fortune from him. He exults in the fact that he cannot read his son's eyes: "'Il sera merveilleux en face des hommes de loi,' pense Brigante. Mais il se garde bien de montrer son ravissement" (140). Aside from not showing any affection, Matteo has trained his son by sending him to law school, by making sure that he has all the material status symbols of the sons of the town notables but without really giving him any spending money, but especially by beating him, not in anger, but methodically, counting or making the boy count the blows. He has always rejoiced that the boy did not whimper, not realizing that this beating is the only real contact Francesco has with his father, that he comes to take pleasure in being beaten, and that he has become a passive, masochistic coward who, like Philippe in _Beau Masque_, is looking for someone to dominate him.

The symbolic ritual of the beating is the game of _La Loi_, a game which, according to the novel, is played in all of southern Italy, and which is a microcosm of the society itself, each player playing for the same reasons he lives--the strong in order to humiliate others, those who have been humiliated in the hope of humiliating someone, and a few simply to pass the time away: "Ce n'est . . . ni l'argent risqué ni le vin bu qui fait l'intérêt du jeu de La Loi, mais la loi elle-même, amère quand on la subit, délectable quand on l'impose" (51). The game can be played with several players; the one match in the novel has six players, which means two winners and four losers. The first phase of the game, the designation of the _patron_, is dispensed with rather rapidly and is the only part of the game involving chance:

> Le gagnant, le patron, qui fait la loi, a le droit de dire et de ne pas dire, d'interroger et de répondre à la place de l'interrogé, de louer et de blâmer, d'injurier, d'insinuer, de médire, de calomnier et de porter atteinte à l'honneur; les perdants, qui subissent la loi, ont le devoir de subir dans le silence et l'immobilité. Telle est la règle fondamentale du jeu de La Loi. (52)

The second phase has a first part in which the _patron_, after a reasonable period of suspense and preliminary insults, chooses a _sous-patron_, and a second part, which is the real game. The losers pay for a liter of wine, seven glasses, and the rest of the game involves seeing who will get to drink the wine.

Obviously the same "rapport de forces" which holds in life will also be present during the game: "Il n'y a pas de jeu qui ne soit régi que par ses propres règles; même dans les jeux de pur hasard, comme la roulette, celui qui n'est pas gêné de perdre a plus de chances de gagner" (57). The game is like life also in that it is not "un jeu selon la justice puisque celui qui n'a qu'un petit capital au départ ne peut pas jouer toutes ses chances" (62). Like any other game and like life, it has spectators who discuss the game and express their approval or disapproval of behavior and strategy. There is disagreement over how the game should be played, but most agree that it is most "plaisante" when there is "une victime, clairement désignée, que le sort et les joueurs traquent jusqu'à épuisement; ainsi seulement ce jeu de pauvres devient aussi excitant que la chasse à courre ou la course de taureaux, davantage même, la victime étant un homme" (72). The reason for the cruelty of the game is that the torturers have also been victims, as exemplified by Tonio waiting his turn "se préparant à faire ravaler leur bile à ses bourreaux, aiguisant les mots qu'il leur lancera. . . . Mais il resta immobile et muet, pétrifié . . . . Il acérait des mots terribles, pour quand viendrait son tour de faire la loi" (60-61). Having been humiliated to the point of physical nausea by the men "playing" in the tavern, Tonio returns home to lord it over the women, who in turn mistreat Mariette, who bides her time waiting for her turn to come. So the cycle continues.

The novel focuses on a certain number of characters exhibiting different stances toward life in this society, most of the names reflecting ironically the distance between a glorious past and the degradation of the present. As in the first four novels particularly, but actually in all the previous novels, each character is a part of Vailland himself, a possible way for him to respond to the world. The characters who lose in the game of the novel are parts of himself which must be destroyed in order to survive, while those who win are parts which must be nurtured.

Alessandro, the judge, is an intellectual, _uomo di cultura_, a "humanist" disillusioned with humanity and with himself, who has ideals about justice but is too weak to fight for them. His lack of virility is seen in his relationship to his car, which is old and neglected, and which he drives very awkwardly. He has malaria and is dominated by his wife, whose infidelity becomes for him a "cas de conscience" (369). He does not go to mass or insist that his wife go, but he does require that his children go to catechism classes for the sake of appearance because of his job and position in this society where church and state are hopelessly entangled. In private he supports the agricultural workers, but in court he condemns them: "Je condamne au minimum" (164).

He is a "magistrat du dernier rang" (6) and has been satisfied to remain just that because for years the great project of his life was a history of Frederick of Swabia, who, although a tyrant, fought against the Pope and his feudal allies and succeeded in imposing a little more justice in southern Italy. Studying his history obviously did not give Alessandro any of his "caractère," and he has abandoned the project. He keeps a _journal intime_, has an old collection of photographs of himself in front of Frederick's castles and palaces and has a new collection of postcards "à sujets," which he calls his "dictionnaire de l'imbécillité" (144), leading him to conclude that if a new Frederick were to appear he would easily procure for each worker a Fiat and a television set: "Alors il n'y aura plus un seul homme assez désoccupé pour réfléchir. L'imbécillité est nécessairement la rançon de la justice" (144-45).

He calls himself a socialist without a party and discusses political theory with Attilio. Ten years previously he had explained to his bride that "pendant des siècles le Sud avait donné des moissons bien au-delà du nécessaire; l'homme avait fleuri, aujourd'hui il végétait, mais puisque le passé avait été différent, le présent pouvait être transformé" (162). But now he is convinced that the future of the South will not be decided in the South, and he reads socialist and Communist periodicals to get some idea of the destiny being prepared elsewhere for his land and its people. The wrap-up at the end of the novel reveals that in his "juste-milieu" position he antagonizes the opposition and the government by "condamnant avec des attendus qui absolvaient" (369) and is sent to a small mountain town in Calabria.

Lucrezia, his wife, is given the title _donna_, although that title is generally reserved for daughters or wives of the great hereditary landowners: "Elle est à l'évidence donna, _domina_ comme l'impératrice des Romains, la maîtresse, la patronne" (6). Raised in a "famille de petite bourgeoisie" in Foggia, where there were fifteen people living in four rooms, she remained "fière, intègre," disgusted by the sexual innuendoes with which she was surrounded, but completely ignorant of love or sex. She attended secondary school, but never took her final examination. She read nineteenth-century French and Italian novels from which she got an idealistic view of passion: "Elle n'avait établi aucun rapport entre l'amour que lui décrivaient des romans lus distraitement et les chienneries auxquelles on ne cessait de faire allusion autour d'elle" (160). She looked upon marriage as a way to escape all the eyes surrounding her so she could find solitude and silence to read "sérieusement." She accepted sexual relations with her husband because that was her lot in life and cared for her children for the same reason.

In the early years of their marriage her husband helped to complete her education, exposing her to ideas of past glory and future progress, encouraging her penchant for reading: "Pendant dix ans, il avait _élevé_ Lucrezia, maintenant qu'elle était _majeure_, elle éprouvait l'impérieux besoin de le quitter; elle détestait son tuteur de lui rappeler sa faiblesse dépassée" (175). Gradually losing respect for her husband and not wishing to submit to him "au nom de la loi," she succeeds in effecting a compromise whereby she can have a room to herself, "mais elle s'engagea à l'y recevoir quelquefois. Il devait, chaque fois, alterner les prières et les sommations" (165).

Thrown into contact with Francesco at social gatherings, she introduces him to La Chartreuse de Parme. He sees her as la Sanseverina and is constrained and "angoissé" in her presence:

> Lucrezia n'avait encore jamais raisonné des humains qu'avec la tête; mais elle avait senti ce silence-là au creux de la poitrine, lieu des angoisses. Lorsqu'en partant Francesco avait un instant retenu sa main, l'angoisse était brusquement tombée dans le ventre. La voilà devenue femme. (173)

She uses the heroines of her readings in order to "l'éclairer sur son sentiment," but acts "dans son style à elle" (174). She exults in being a woman like other women, in having a passion, continually repeating to herself: "J'aime Francesco Brigante" (174). It is she who arranges their one meeting, after which she is grateful to him for his "délicatesse," in not requiring her to submit to any "chienneries." It is she who makes the plans and the arrangements for their future life together in the north and who gives him the money to set up an apartment, planning all she will do for him: "Je ferai son bonheur" (174). When she learns that he has lost the money in a brothel, she is only too willing to take him back, declaring her love to the whole town; he, however, thinking she despises him, slinks home to his father. Once awakened to her sexual nature, she has an affair with Attilio, the first of a long line of affairs: "Toujours hautaine, elle méprisait la prudence. On ne dit plus d'elle donna Lucrezia, mais la Lucrezia" (369).

Francesco, raised in a home with no affection, trained to present an impassive face to the world, actually resembles his passive, submissive mother more than his father. A law student because of his father's ambition for him, his one real interest is music and his electric guitar. What he is looking for in Lucrezia and in anyone is comfort, release from the eternal façade and from fear. Shy, without much spending money, considering "nice" girls beyond his reach, knowing love only in hurried visits to brothels, he is given to daydreams, but he is convinced the girls in his daydreams are only "un avant-goût des femmes véritables" (156). He thinks he has found such a woman in Lucrezia, who is older, seems at ease, and talks about literature.

> Ses gestes échappent . . . à toute prévision, donnant l'impression qu'elle ne se meut que pour son plaisir à elle, sans se soucier des autres. Elle se déplace comme coule le torrent, selon sa loi propre.
>
> Il n'avait encore jamais rencontré une femme qui eût une nature et qui se comportait avec naturel. (157)

After she introduces him to Stendhal and other French novelists, he is caught in the trap of romantic love, sees her as a heroine, and exults in the fact that he is in love and has a "maîtresse," even though they have not shared so much as a kiss. She begins to appear in his nightmares; for years he has had a dream of being chased by his father; now his pursuer has an ambiguous face and "les yeux froids et impérieux de son père, les yeux brûlants et impérieux de sa maîtresse, les yeux froids-brûlants de son père et de sa maîtresse" (183). Alone with her in the cavern he is uncomfortable, not knowing what to do, wondering what his "devoir" is, while she thinks how at ease he is, what a true man he is, etc. As the trap closes on the fish in the <u>trabucco</u>, they remain in a chaste embrace like mother and child. As he relaxes for the first time in his life, his words are "Sainte Mère de Dieu" (209). Later, leaving town on the bus, he wears the conservative clothing she had instructed him to wear, knowing she will be looking from her window and wishing to make her happy "en se montrant par avance docile à suivre ses conseils" (294), but carrying in his suitcase a change of clothes more to his taste. Taken to the brothel by his father, he is ministered to by a girl who knows her "métier"; in gratitude he gives her Lucrezia's money and, just as his father had planned, comes home "la queue entre les jambes" (310).

In the "game" of this novel, and in all of Vailland's novels, Alessandro, Lucrezia, and Francesco and their relationship to life are losers, as are the parts of Vailland himself incarnated in them. Don Cesare, like Lamballe and Valerio Empoli, is not actually a player, possessing an excess of power which he rarely uses. The richest landowner in the area, he is seventy-two years old and has outlived his time. He lives in the "maison à colonnades" beside the swamp with Julia, who was once his mistress, and her daughters, Maria, who was also his mistress and is now Tonio's wife; Elvire, who is now his mistress; and Mariette, who is a virgin. He has complete control of the women when he is present, but he actually has no conception of what goes on when he is absent. When he chooses to use it, he has complete power over the police and the judge. All his business affairs are in the hands of managers, who all cheat him; he knows this and occasionally fires one of them at random to show that he is not taken in. Although he detests motorized vehicles of all kinds, his virility is never questioned because his sexual prowess is now legendary.

He has been "en retraite" for forty years and spends his time hunting in the marshes and collecting artifacts from the Greek city of Uria brought to him by "his" fishermen. His history and map of the city have been finished for years and are lying in a drawer because he does not want to be bothered with editing and dealing with publishers. He was "formé" by his reading of Vico, and early in his retirement, like every _uomo di cultura_, he made up his own philosophy of history based on recurring cycles of theocratic, heroic, and democratic ages with the heroic age of the kings as the apogee. He decides that he was born "sur la mauvaise pente de l'éternel retour" (91).

From his deathbed he looks back over his life and remembers 1946 as the year his great niece delighted him by defying his caresses, causing him to invite her to Porto Manacore in the hope that she could be "une collaboratrice intelligente" (90). But she showed no curiosity about his artifacts and, unknown to him, was so hounded by the other women in the household that she came to his bed at night. For these reasons he calls her "la petite-nièce qui ne s'était pas maintenue dans sa fierté" (91). As with all his relatives, he uses to judge her a standard of conduct, a code of honor, completely divorced from the concrete realities with which she lives. That was the same year Umberto II lost his throne and the year which succeeded in convincing him that "la servilité humaine n'a pas de limite" (93). He is now "désintéressé . . . une grande statue qui marcherait inlassablement, du même grand pas mécanique" (104).

> Ses paroles résonnent dans un monde sans écho; ses gestes se développent dans un espace sans consistance. (105)
> Il se tenait là, dans son fauteuil à accoudoirs tourneboulés, immobile, attentif, dans l'attente pesante de quelque événement qu'il savait ne pas devoir se produire. (93)

He still does, by habit, the things he has always done and expresses a kind of interest in the Greek artifacts, recognizing that only in death can one be absolutely disinterested. But he is so disinterested that he has become an object for himself:

> Don Cesare en face de don Cesare pensant la statuette de terre cuite et l'intelligente cité d'Uria, mais aussi étranger à don Cesare qu'à la statuette de terre cuite et à la morte cité d'Uria; sans amour, sans haine, sans plus aucun désir d'aimer ou de haïr, aussi dépourvu de toute sorte de désir que la défunte cité d'Uria. (109)

It seems, however, that seeing himself as an object is another long-standing habit. On his deathbed he tells Mariette of an affair he had just after World War I when "il est arrivé qu'une femme me fît la loi" (348). Caught in a web of passion, jealousy, and humiliation, he one day for no apparent reason suddenly realized "qu'il ne subissait plus sa loi" and in that moment he saw himself and the woman as he would have seen two actors on a stage: "Il avait regardé avec étonnement Lucienne et cet homme qui avait aimé Lucienne à la passion, lui et elle, deux étrangers désormais" (350). Looking back he sees this as the first of the "refus successifs sur lesquels il avait édifié sa vie" (351). He had been a drunk and a gambler, but one day he saw himself as a stranger and he ceased to be that man and stopped gambling.

Drinking was more difficult to alienate, so difficult, in fact, that he was unable to do it alone and was forced to enlist the aid of a doctor:

> Aussitôt apaisés les spasmes du sevrage, analogues aux convulsions du nouveau-né, comme un fruit dont on vient d'arracher l'écorce, nu pour la première fois dans la lumière, le froid, les bruits et les attouchements, aussitôt dégorgés les humeurs de la mue, il fut comme mort. (352)

Identifying the clouds he saw from his bed with his own death, he realized that he must be alive if he could see his own death. He thus began to cherish life once more. Politics was the most difficult passion to overcome; when Victor Emmanuel allowed real power to be taken over by Mussolini, don Cesare was once again "comme mort" for more than a year.

The reason for his successive refusals, his morality, "la règle intransgressible de toute sa vie" was that he was saving himself for the really great, important task:

> Chaque fois qu'il s'était trouvé sur le point d'être complètement _engagé_ dans ce qu'il sentait ne pas être cette tâche essentielle (qu'il n'avait finalement jamais eu à accomplir) il avait brusquement et aisément dégagé, comme dégage un escrimeur bien né et entraîné aux armes. (351-52)

After the _buffone_ (Mussolini; Khrushchev) replaced the _baffone_ (Victor Emmanuel; Stalin) on the throne and don Cesare returned to the land of the living, "il n'avait plus jamais identifié sa raison de vivre avec la tâche entreprise" (354). On his deathbed he reviews ancient and modern history and his own history, convinced that he has committed suicide "lentement, par phases successives, à la mesure de son époque" (357) and that the quality of "un homme de qualité" resides in this succession of engagements and disengagements, in this movement itself. He decides that he has lived the only way a man of quality could live in a time and a country which made it necessary to commit suicide slowly, "mais non sans plaisirs," in order not to destroy his quality.

His deathbed thoughts are his witness of himself to himself: "Il a été ainsi. Il ne regrette rien; il n'a honte de rien; il ne désire plus rien; il se reconnaît, il se proclame (à lui-même) tel qu'il a été et tel qu'il demeure à l'heure de sa mort" (355). There is no one else to whom he could bear this witness. Mariette, physically present at his death, views him as God the Father, God the Son, and God the Holy Spirit: "Il aurait préféré semblable à Zeus, à Phébus, et à Hermès, mais c'était l'autre mythologie qu'on avait enseignée à Mariette" (339). As a god he has no friends and no real contact with human beings. Since the age of twenty he has spent every night of his life with a woman in bed with him to have a body to touch before going to sleep. Even the insensitive Elvire wonders if he knows "que c'est elle, Elvire, qu'il est en train de prendre" (104). Women have been for him a continuing source of pleasure: "L'antique ville d'Uria avait été consacrée à Vénus; le dernier seigneur d'Uria, après avoir durant des années arraché au sable et aux marais les vestiges de la noble cité, mourait du mal de Vénus; sa vie s'achevait sans dissonance" (334-35). The doctor's reaction to this statement and the repudiation of this view of life in _Un Jeune Homme Seul_ serve to put ironic distance between Vailland and don Cesare.

On his deathbed he experiences more emotion than he has felt in years when he discovers what Mariette is really like. He is "enchanted" and "delighted" to discover that she is "intransigeante comme un bandit d'honneur. Inaccessible à la crainte" (344). He is delighted to discover that there are still "des enfants hardis dans cette Italie qu'il avait crue n'être plus préoccupée que de scooters et de télévision" (342). Fortunately for both of them, he dies before he gets a chance to take her as his mistress as he has done the other women in her family. Like the *deus ex machina* which he is, he leaves her a fortune and dies with his hand on her breast, realizing he is the last person to see the world as he sees it: "Plus personne ne sera jamais capable d'envelopper dans un seul regard tout ce passé et ce présent, ce passé de l'histoire des hommes et de l'histoire d'un homme étroitement unis dans le présent solennellement présent d'un homme en train de mourir en pleine lucidité" (363).

The future belongs to the winners, to those who can adapt to their environment and to the system in such a way that in the eyes of the public they wield more power than they are forced to submit to; the future belongs to Attilio, to Matteo Brigante, and to Mariette. Attilio is the police commissioner, and the police always win in this kind of society, but he is not a big winner because he is salaried and will have to be promoted to a larger town if he really wants money and prestige. His only slim hope of escape is the personal influence of people like a woman his wife has met at the beach, "une Romaine, amie intime de la nièce d'un cardinal" (44). His pleasure in life is possessing women, especially married women. He shows himself to be a caricature of the "libertin" of the Valmont variety, taking great pride in initiating the "rupture," but allowing the affair to go on after the "rupture." During most of the novel he is "possédé" by Giuseppina, "la vierge folle," but he escapes relatively unscathed, thanks to his discovery of the possibility of "possessing" Lucrezia. It is evident that he is himself possessed by the need to "have" the game which he hunts down without much effort because of the facilities offered by his job and his position.

Attilio and Matteo both have in general the same idea of love: "Ce qui lui donne du prix, c'est de faire la loi à l'autre, femme ou jeune fille" (236). For actual physical pleasure the girls in the brothels are more expert than anyone else, even though this kind of sex is not as exciting as it is to "faire la loi à une amante" (236). There are cases in which the girls in the brothels can surpass other girls; by paying, the customer "fait la loi"; but by requiring payment, the girl "fait la loi." Thus a skillful prostitute can keep ever present this "double dépendance-liberté" (236-37). Without the presence of "la loi" Attilio and Matteo both agree there only remains the physical pleasure, which they can get from a goat, or alone, or with their wives, who are so accustomed to submission that it is not really worth the trouble to make them submit.

Attilio prefers to pay court to wives of notables, to surround them with attention, exhaust himself in bed persuaded he is giving them pleasure they cannot find with their husbands: "Quand Attilio s'est enfin persuadé que son amante lui appartient sans réserve, il lui apprend les gestes, les poses, les pratiques des filles de Foggia. 'Je la dégrade,' dit-il. Puis il rompt et passe à une autre" (238). Matteo thinks Attilio is actually doing their husbands a favor, teaching the wives how to make the husband happier in the future; in any case, he sees Attilio's way as too cerebral for his tastes or for his position in the hierarchy.

Matteo Brigante is the son of an agricultural worker who has sworn never to be an agricultural worker. He "controls" Porto Manacore, receiving ten per cent of everything that happens in town. The only segment of society which he does not control is that composed of Pippo's street gang, whose freedom is a function of the fact that they have nothing and what they steal is consumed immediately. Matteo has invested his money in different ways, in the olive oil industry, in the transportation of bauxite, in land speculation, in houses of prostitution. He now makes more money from his investments than from his control of Porto Manacore.

Matteo has the "regard froid" and the habit of reflecting of Marat in _Drôle de Jeu_, turning in thought around a fact until he finds an analogy which clarifies the whole. He, unlike Marat, believes strongly in God and "la Sainte Église" because society as he knows it is irrefutable proof of the existence of God at the top of the hierarchy. The only reason he has to commit so many sins is that God permitted him to become controller of Porto Manacore, but not a member of the higher classes of society. Matteo is much richer than Attilio, but everywhere except in the "garçonnière" they share he must call him "monsieur le commissaire" and use the formal address, while Attilio can call him Brigante and use informal address. To enjoy the privileges to which he thinks his fortune should entitle him, he would have to leave Porto Manacore. But even this is not certain. Watching the seemingly rich tourists in their large cars he sometimes wonders whether they in their own countries are not really quartermasters like him trying to give themselves the illusion of being superior officers:

> Du fond de la _trattoria_, Matteo Brigante les épie; il guette le geste, le ton, le manque de désinvolture ou la trop grande désinvolture qui feront la preuve que l'étranger est un tricheur, comme il sera lui-même tricheur s'il s'exile. Le Brigante de l'endroit où il s'exilera découvrira tout de suite qu'il est tricheur. Dans le monde de Dieu, on n'échappe pas aux contrôleurs que Dieu a placés un peu partout et qui, en prélevant leur dîme sur le désordre, contribuent à leur manière au maintien de l'ordre. (232)

Matteo's choices were limited when he was young, caught in the hierarchy with God at the top and the agricultural worker at the bottom, "le mal-être absolu" (242); other conceptions of society, which "supposent la lecture de journaux et de livres, ou tout au moins la fréquentation de lecteurs de journaux et de livres" (243), were impossible for Matteo. Since only God escapes having someone give him orders and only the agricultural workers have no one to give orders to, the only solution is to move up from the bottom of the ladder; "Subir la loi, soit; mais aussi faire la loi; ainsi l'enfant conçut-il la dignité humaine" (243).

Now his favorite pasttime is raping virgins, which he calls "exécution," and which he considers makes him more virile than Attilio. Unlike Attilio he does not have to make a plan of seduction in advance because the plan is always the same; neither does he take time to taste his pleasure in advance: "Son plaisir . . . est un plaisir de l'instant, absolu, dont on ne peut donc se délecter à l'avance (sauf en le racontant en public, en présence de quelqu'un qui en souffre)" (247). His plan is simple: "Il fit encore deux pas et la gifla à toute volée, une fois sur chaque joue. C'est ainsi qu'il procède. On ne peut rien sur une vierge récalcitrante si d'abord on ne l'assomme pas" (251). His weopon is brute strength with the aim of producing fear and surrender. When Mariette makes use of his own philosophy of man's triumph over nature (using the wind to sail against the wind) by exhibiting no fear and attacking him with his own knife, he is confused and retreats ignomoniously. Attempting to negotiate with her through the closed door, his voice softens and becomes "presque tendre," recognizing in her a partner worthy of him: "La méchanceté, où il croyait avoir trouvé la source de sa propre force, lui inspirait toujours du respect chez lui et chez les autres" (281).

At the end of the novel Matteo is optimistic about the future even though Francesco has just failed his law examinations for the third time. His wife has just had her third operation for breast cancer, and he has visions of marrying Mariette, who is, according to everyone except her mother, the daughter of don Cesare. Together they will rule the town financially and socially; "elective affinities" have become animal instinct, and the "Pléïade" has become the Mafia.

Mariette is a more elemental creature than any of the other protagonists, as shown by her gift of _la voix_ and her ability to maneuver boats in the swamps without disturbing the aquatic birds. Her childhood in the "maison à colonnades" of don Cesare was very primitive, the women fighting among themselves like animals. Mariette and other girls are looked upon by the men in the tavern as livestock and are compared to goats, which the men also use for sexual pleasure. Her adolescence is spent surrounded by the cruelty of her mother and sisters and by men everywhere making obscene remarks and trying to touch her. Her reaction, as she looks at the world with "le regard dur," is: "Mon tour viendra" (147). She is sixteen years old and scarcely knows how to read and write, but elementary strategy does not require literacy. Before Matteo comes to the shed to try to rape her, she is engaged in thought, using pieces of straw "comme les pièces d'un échiquier, les déplaçant sur ses genoux, personnages imaginaires, symboles d'obstacles et d'aides. Elle combine un plan à longue échéance, utilisant les brins de paille comme un comptable son boulier" (246-47). Her actions when Matteo attacks her are those of a "noble savage" defending itself against an enemy whose habits and strengths it knows. Her attitude and expression while she advances on Matteo and marks him with the knife are described in the same terms as those describing Le Bressan cycling uphill against the curtain of rain in _325.000 francs_.

In contrast to the meeting of Lucrezia and Francesco in the cavern near the _trabucco_ with its connotations of being caught in a trap, devoured by the monster, or returned to the womb, and in contrast to Francesco's visit to the brothel, where the décor and the personnel remind him of an elegant clinic, Mariette and Pippo, "le romantique chef de brigands" with "un regard de flamme et de tendresse" (351), meet in the Garden of Eden, the earthly paradise before literary or Christian influences, "dans le jardin aux sources . . . dans le murmure des eaux vives, dans le parfum des fleurs qui préparent les fruits d'hiver tandis que déjà se dorent les fruits de l'automne" (148). Before this they have been together frequently, have told each other of their love, and plan to marry, but "ils n'avaient encore jamais échangé ni caresses, ni même baisers de bouche" (274) simply because they have never wanted to. In their lovemaking, which happens "naturally," they are described as pagan: "Ils se retrouvèrent exactement semblables aux pâtres des collines voisines de la prospère cité d'Uria" (277). Mariette is described as "fondamentalement païenne," which is considered good in that she avoids the concepts of sin, guilt, resignation, and submission. She is, however, highly superstitious, continually making "les cornes avec l'index et l'auriculaire" to ward off evil spirits.

Her unpremeditated act of exchanging Matteo's billfold and the one stolen from the Swiss couple is examined by several characters. The explanation of her motives ranges from Matteo's view that it was a conspiratorial wink asking for future aid from a man of experience and maturity, to her own explanation to don Cesare that she was pleased with herself and making fun of Matteo. The explanation for her behavior is not formulated until La Truite. In La Loi it is seen as an instinctive action with positive results. The novel ends with Mariette ensconced in the "maison à colonnades," furnished with "des meubles modernes en contreplaqué verni" (371). She has a Fiat 400 and a television set and plans with the help of Matteo "un hôtel, un restaurant, une station-service, des villas, un ensemble touristique, expression qu'elle avait entendue à la télévision" (376). With Matteo's financial help and instruction in "les techniques modernes de nage sous-marine" (372), Pippo spends the profitable tourist season on the islands and returns to Mariette during the off season.

The three of them might well echo the words of Mme Lemercier at the end of *325.000 francs*: "Nous serons pas mal à l'aise" (244).

In *Drôle de Jeu*, *Les Mauvais Coups*, *Un Jeune Homme Seul*, the winners were characters with whom Vailland and the *persona* Marat-Lamballe could identify and whose relationship to the world was acceptable at that time. In *Beau Masque* he himself was a winner and could accept the positions of the other winners. In *325.000 francs* he was once more in the novel, which offset the fact that Jambe d'Argent and Jules Morel were the winners. *La Loi* is like *Bon Pied Bon Oeil* in that within the novel there is no character who represents an acceptable position for the *persona* which has been defining itself throughout all the novels. The character who comes closest is don Cesare, who died because he had obviously outlived his time. But, like don Cesare, who knew he was alive because he saw his own death, Vailland, by seeing his own death in don Cesare, knows that he is alive and presents *La Loi* as proof of that fact. Like Marat, he did not commit suicide and has survived into another time, but Marat had a war to fight. The problem is now how to survive with dignity when there are no wars "l'esprit libre" can fight.

THE NOVELIST

La Fête, published in 1960, is a novel written in the third person by an omniscient narrator about a writer who is writing a novel. *La Fête*, more than *La Loi*, is the future novel referred to by Vailland in a letter written 21 May, 1956: "Je crois que je serais maintenant capable d'écrire un livre sur moi-même, ce qui, à mon âge et après les précédents livres, est bien le comble du détachement de soi" (*Écrits Intimes* 483). Explicit and implicit references to works such as Vigny's *Stello* and Sartre's *Qu'est-ce que la Littérature?* identify the novel as an exploration of the situation of the writer and at the same time place Vailland's personal history in a framework of literary history at least as much as in that of "history." That the protagonist is intended to be Vailland is indicated by the similarity of biographical details and by the almost verbatim transcription of pages from his *Choses vues en Égypte*, published in 1952. The novel explores the concept of "souveraineté," which Milan said Roberte had taken from him, and examines once more the problems of freedom in love and marriage as first exposed in *Les Mauvais Coups*.

The structure of the novel is circular, beginning and ending with the same words:

> Duc, après un long voyage, venait de regagner sa maison de campagne, non loin des rives de la Saône; il commençait d'écrire un roman; c'est son métier. Léone, sa femme, pour préserver la paix nécessaire à son travail, répondait au téléphone qu'il n'était pas encore revenu. Un soir, on sonna à leur porte, elle attendait un fournisseur, elle ouvrit. (7)

The plot line is very simple. Jean-Marc Lemarque, an aspiring poet who does "de petits travaux d'amateur" (51), and his wife, Lucie, who has a regular office job in Paris, stop to visit an older couple, Duc, who is a writer, and his wife Léone, who takes care of Duc and their home. Duc is writing a novel, which is not going well because he is bored. He is attracted to Lucie and arranges for the young couple to return the following weekend, at which time he and Lucie declare their love for each other. He and Lucie spend the next weekend together in an inn about an hour's drive from his home; she returns to Paris, her husband, and her job; he returns to his wife and the new novel which he will write after abandoning the one he was working on at the beginning, inaugurating what Léone calls "la saison du roman qui n'en est pas un" (284).

At the end of the novel, just as he is beginning to write the new one, Duc tells Léone what his plan is and what the themes are which he wants to develop:

> D'abord un long chapitre, lourd, massif, entièrement écrit au présent, la promenade dans le bois avec Jean-Marc et Lucie; j'y pose les thèmes que j'ai envie de développer; la souveraineté, l'amour fou, la fête, les moyens d'expression de l'écrivain et les rapports de l'homme et de l'automobile. (284)

A second reading of the novel shows that it does not quite follow the plan set up by Duc at the end, but these are certainly the themes of the novel. The discussion in the first chapter among Lucie, Jean-Marc, and Duc about the novel he is writing could easily form the basis for an academic course called "The Craft of Fiction" and introduces the game which is the novel *La Fête*. Rather than a game, the novel is compared to a race, where going the distance is the aim. To Jean-Marc's insistence that weighing a concept like sovereignty should be done in an essay rather than in a novel, Duc answers: "Un *essai* ne fait jamais le poids. Les coureurs font des essais avant la course; moi, c'est la course qui m'intéresse" (26). The successful completion of the race, the novel, does for Vailland and for Duc what Duc said any novel he wrote at this time would do, that is, give "mon poids dans le moment où j'écris, le poids d'un homme à la recherche de sa souveraineté" (34).

Duc is not don Cesare, who was completely disinterested. Lucie comments on the fact that Duc wants to do so many things: "Aucun de nos amis n'a autant de désirs que toi" (38). Duc sees himself thus:

> De sa propre histoire, il est assez dégagé maintenant--quoique continuant de vivre intensément, c'est-à-dire d'avoir des désirs et de les satisfaire--pour en avoir une vision d'ensemble, une vue comme de l'extérieur, capable maintenant de réfléchir sur sa propre histoire comme sur n'importe quoi qui lui serait étranger mais qui l'intéresserait. (164-65)

In addition, Duc is a writer, which don Cesare was not. As he writes his novel, he realizes why the character whom he calls the docteur cannot be his porte-parole. The doctor left a family and a profitable practice in Paris to become a ship's doctor and resident humanist and sage: "Il y a entre le docteur et lui une différence essentielle: le docteur n'écrit pas de romans; il ne peut pas parler comme Duc, pour Duc" (63). Lucie had already realized the importance of this fact when Duc was telling her and Jean-Marc about the novel and the older character who resembled him, but was not a writer: "Alors . . . ce n'est pas toi" (24).

The basic distinction between the sage and the writer is emphasized from the beginning. Duc is not a "collectionneur," but he knows women and he knows plants. Knowing, as Jean-Marc tells Lucie, "c'est formidable pour lui" (16). But a writer is not satisfied with knowing; he must be able to express in words what he knows and what he feels:

> C'est ce rapport qui fait la réalité de cette plante, ce rapport multiple et unique de matière et de forme, je sens ce rapport, je le sens, comme dirait Lucie, et si je savais l'exprimer avec des mots . . . si je savais exprimer ce rapport, cette réalité, ne serait-ce qu'avec des images, une série d'images qui l'encerclent complètement, je serais un grand écrivain. (16)

This process of expressing the "rapport exact" is discussed in terms of weighing an object, finding "le poids juste" (19); in this context Lucie is compared to a weighing scale: "Une très précieuse balance . . . . Lucie a un don tout à fait exceptionnel pour distinguer le vrai du faux, l'authentique du truqué et elle ne met jamais aucune complaisance dans l'énoncé de son jugement" (19). Duc insists that he can also "faire le poids d'une idée": "Une idée, c'est aussi réel qu' orchis bifolia ou que les yeux de Lucie" (25). He wants to "faire le poids de la souveraineté" (25) because he does not know what it is, but: "Je le saurai quand mon roman sera achevé et si mon roman est réussi" (26). The novel is the instrument wherein and whereby Duc weighs himself in relation to the world, but especially in relation to Lucie. She is seen as the adolescent "pas tout à fait sortie du cocon, accomplissant à tâtons son premier vol, avec encore des soies accrochées aux facettes de ses yeux, se cognant à chaque objet dans son inventaire pathétique du monde" (11). In relation to Duc, Léone, Jean-Marc, and Alexandre, who seem to be "quatre solennelles statues de pierre" (220), Lucie "prend feu. . . . Elle flambe, c'est une flamme" (108). The problem is to see the flame without being dazzled by it, to play with fire without being burned; to see Lucie as an object and experience "l'amour fou" with her at the same time; to find a middle ground between "La Mort du Loup" of Alfred de Vigny and the poetry of Alfred de Musset.

The novel shows that the craft of writing is one of the principal attributes of Duc's sovereignty and the one which makes him morally equal or superior when weighed in a balance with the other characters in the novel. The amateur-professional dichotomy is in this novel a dichotomy between the amateur and the "écrivain de métier," who is following his vocation. The combination of vocation and métier is seen in the ambiguity of the name Duc, a name which, through a play on words not apparent in English, implies the moral superiority of Duc over Milan and Busard. As the bird, he is a bird of prey whose natural calling is to be a writer; as the duke he is a civilized nobleman who uses the métier of writing as the noblemen of a somewhat romanticized past used war.

The difference between Jean-Marc, who also has the vocation to be a writer, but who works _en amateur_, and Duc, who accepts the discipline of the métier, is seen in another play on words during the discussion between Duc and Jean-Marc concerning the girl in Marseilles who was embroidering. She was not working "sur un métier": "Elle faisait des jours. . . . C'est moins magnifique, mais c'est tout de même très gentil" (123). His amateur status and his "gentillesse" are seen as two components of a personality structure and attitude toward life characterized by a lack of virility. He drives slowly and with "nonchalance" a "quatre-chevaux . . . cabossée en maints endroits, l'âge des bosses lisible dans l'écaillure de la peinture et les nuances variées des mastiquages" (102); Duc drives a D.S., which he keeps in perfect condition and which he uses to challenge other drivers on the highway. Jean-Marc has many ideas about literary theory and technique, but has never written anything with which he is satisfied; Duc is a successful novelist and puts his ideas into practice. Jean-Marc is satisfied with taking money from his parents and from his wife; Duc is financially independent. Jean-Marc considers his wife his "maison": "Il l'a édifiée, il l'a faite à l'image de lui-même, sa femme, sa maison, le plus intime de lui-même" (209). Duc constructs himself; outside himself he begins at the end of the novel transforming an old stable into "une retraite pour l'amour" (209), emphasizing his mobility within stability. Léone describes Jean-Marc: "Tu ne sais ni défendre, ni prendre" (210). Duc carries out and completes successfully a carefully-planned military campaign: "Duc attaqua Lucie dans la matinée" (144).

Duc is also seen to be in a better position than his father-in-law, Alexandre, who is obviously a sovereign who has devoted his life to being an "amateur de femmes," but who is now seventy-two years old and for the first time is afraid women will not be attracted to him: "Quand une jeune femme lui paraissait désirable, il la cajolait, comme il avait toujours fait, mais il n'osait pas attaquer, préoccupé de l'idée que certaines femmes se font de la vieillesse, ou, peut-être, redoutant ses propres défaillances" (226). Léone recognizes that her father still has his sovereignty, "qui est maîtrise et possession de soi-même," but she realizes that he is losing "l'attribut le plus glorieux de sa souveraineté" (226). She tells Duc: "Toi, tu écris des livres, d'autres s'amusent à changer la face du monde. À soixante-douze ans, les grands politiques sont dans la verdeur de l'âge. Alexandre, lui, n'a que l'amour qu'il porte aux femmes et qu'elles lui portaient" (226).

Duc also weighs more than the three young professors whom he had known in the days of political fervor:

> Maintenant, ils faisaient du cinéma en amateur avec une caméra de 16 millimètres . . . . Un grand nombre de jeunes gens, ces années-là, rêvaient de réaliser un court métrage, à propos de n'importe quoi, mais dans lequel ils s'exprimeraient tout entiers. (191)

La Fête is the same kind of undertaking although Duc, unlike his friends, is not young. His undertaking, however, carries more "weight" because he is not an amateur but an "écrivain de métier" with a reputation and a public awaiting his next novel. In addition the depth and breadth of objective reality represented in the work carries more "weight" than theirs. The professors had been filming "des sous-bois, dans une forêt de sapins" (191); Duc is the focus of *La Fête* as he interacts with the flora of the region, with the people with whom he comes in contact, with the world of Parisian officeworkers and of political activists in Egypt, with his own past history, and with the history and reality of the novel as a genre.

Duc tells Jean-Marc and Lucie that:

> Il avait pensé que c'était sur le bolchevik qu'il devait se modeler, s'il voulait vraiment vivre son temps, et que c'était lui qu'il devait peindre, dans toute sa réalité, s'il voulait faire une oeuvre durable, c'est-à-dire qui exprime, dans son essence, le monde de son temps. (176)

He thus gives equal emphasis to living his time and expressing it in a work. Believing himself "à l'extrême pointe du siècle" he had discovered "que l'Histoire était entrée dans une nouvelle phase, sans qu'il s'en fût aperçu" (176). Now he does not know what the "homme nouveau" is like: "Il est très difficile de penser l'Histoire au jour le jour. Il faut faire retraite, prendre distance" (176-77). This distance is not complete separation. Although he rarely reads the newspapers, he does stop to buy a weekly paper before looking for a suitable setting for his week-end with Lucie and decides that "rien de ce qui se passait dans le monde, en ce mois de juin 1959, ne lui semblait exiger, à tort ou à raison, d'être pris à coeur par lui" (231). He still receives echoes from his days of political action. It is a Communist bulletin, Solidarité, which informs him of the imprisonment and torture of his friend Kamal, but Kamal is on his mind before the arrival of this news. One of the problems faced in the novel is Duc's public image and self-esteem when comparing his present situation of non-combattant with that of Kamal and of Lucie: "Kamal est de nouveau en prison et Lucie prend le métro; ils ne sont pas libres de cesser le combat" (99). It is actually left up to present and future readers of the novel to judge what Duc and La Fête weigh in the balance with these two, just as within the novel the repeated discussions of Mark Antony's leaving the battle of Actium to follow Cleopatra elucidate his personal reasons and the historical consequences, but do not reach a definitive conclusion because each person uses a different scale.

Duc looks at his experiences in Egypt seven years prior to the time of the novel to try to understand them and the feeling of fraternity which he had then and which he regrets. He realizes that even at the height of what he then considered a fraternal experience every individual was using that experience for his own purposes. Looking back over his life, he realizes that he has always used people and situations to his own ends as they have used him: "Il est même possible que je n'aie pris--à diverses occasions--le risque d'aller en prison, de me faire tuer ou d'être torturé, que pour me faire à moi-même la preuve de ma souveraineté sur moi-mêeme. La preuve faite, mes guerres sont terminées" (99). He tells Jean-Marc and Lucie how friends and enemies alike tried to take advantage of his imprisonment in Egypt and how he remembers himself in that situation:

> Duc a les larmes aux yeux. Il se voit attaché à la chaîne des forçats, sous les yeux du peuple compatissant, comme les déportés en Sibérie, du temps des tsars, il se voit par les yeux de Dostoïevsky [sic] et de Gorki. Il fait belle figure dans son monde romanesque. Et il se demande aussitôt comment il racontera cela, comme il l'écrira. (172-73)

When Lucie insists that he was playing a scene, he says that he was reacting as a writer: "Quand un écrivain est dans le malheur, il cherche d'abord les mots pour décrire le malheur, et par là même il y échappe. Écrivain, inapte au malheur" (173).

To Lucie's shock at the way Kamal used him as an object to exploit the situation, Duc answers that he was using himself as an object, too, in order to prove to himself that he would not give in under torture. Although he was not tortured, he thought he was going to be and expected it: "Mais cela lui donna de l'estime pour soi-même, pour son sang, pour ce que les hommes de jadis appelaient leur sang, d'avoir été persuadé, dans cet instant-là, que la colère l'emporterait" (175). He explains to Jean-Marc and Lucie the basic contradiction of any system of morality:

> Il est absurde de mourir pour quelque chose, laquelle chose, pour soi, est abolie dans l'instant même où l'on meurt; mais on ne vit pas intégralement, on ne s'éprouve pas, on ne se trempe pas, on ne se fait pas, on ne mûrit pas, on n'écrit pas sa propre histoire, on ne devient pas souverain, si on ne se prouve pas, dans un certain nombre de circonstances, qu'on est capable de mourir pour quelque chose. (177)

The problem then becomes what to do after having proven himself. Duc insists that he is not a moralist, but "un homme de devoir" continually asking himself what he ought to do or ought not to do and finding his answer in each particular case "à tâtons" (224). Reading the <u>Méditations</u> of Marcus Aurelius, he finds this passage which he considers relevant to himself: "Il faut composer ta vie action par action et si chacune d'elles atteint sa fin propre, dans la mesure du possible, te déclarer satisfait" (225).

For Duc any action must take place within the context of sovereignty. He explains to Jean-Marc and Lucie how he started thinking along these lines when he met a career diplomat who spent his life in negotiations which always ended in compromise, but who was intransigent as to protocol because, as representative of France, he was actually France in those negotiations. Realizing that his own sovereignty is inalienable, Duc has taken this fact as a basis for action: "Je pris la décision, quoi qu'il pût advenir, de ne pas me décider par passion ni par amitié mais politiquement, de puissance à puissance, à l'égard de n'importe quelle puissance dans le monde. Maintenant je dirais: de souverain à souverain" (28). He uses the lion and the wolf as examples of sovereigns and the dog, as in <u>Les Mauvais Coups</u>, as an animal who has abdicated his sovereignty to his master. He believes he and Léone are now sovereigns: "C'est le fruit d'une longue suite de guerres, pour chacun de nous, que nous avons livrées à la terre entière, et chacun à soi-même, d'année en année, pendant beaucoup d'années" (30). But he and Léone have never engaged in battle with each other because when they met they had "achevé de vider nos querelles" (53). He compares them to two seventeenth-century generals who know how to live: "Chacun se renseigne sur les forces de l'adversaire, ses positions, son ravitaillement, ses possibilités de manoeuvres, le moral de ses troupes. Quand ils savent tout cela, la bataille est devenue inutile" (54). After a series of prudent advances and retreats, "la saison de la guerre" has finished.

Duc says he and Léone are actually more intelligent and more experienced than the generals because they recognize the futility of war itself and respect each other "comme des rois égaux" (55). They never quarrel, Léone because she claims she never wants to and Duc because he laughs at himself before he really begins. They think out loud with each other:

> C'était un des fondements de leur entente que cette réflexion en commun sur ce qu'ils voyaient, sur ce qu'ils ressentaient, sur les hommes et les femmes qui venaient chez eux. Ils ne discutaient pas, ils ne disputaient pas, ils s'aidaient à clarifier, à préciser leurs idées, leurs sentiments. Ils ne cherchaient absolument pas à gagner l'un sur l'autre, ni même à convaincre, seulement à élucider. (79)

Like equal kings, they are not completely open with each other; Léone does not tell Duc how bad she thinks his novel is until he has decided to abandon it, and Duc does not tell her that he wants to love Lucie and not simply be loved by her: "Ce que je suis gentil moi aussi" (143). The salient characteristic of sovereigns is that they are genteel and civilized.

Observing himself and the others listening to records, Duc thinks: "Nous sommes bien élevés . . . nous sommes tous bien élevés, ce que nous sommes bien élevés. Je n'ai pas été bien élevé, je n'étais pas bien élevé" (136). But he behaves as if he had been "bien élevé" in order to treat others as sovereigns. It is evident that his "gentillesse" is a result of a careful weighing of the situation and of alternative courses of action, not simply as a blind following of rules: "Maintenant il sait se contrôler" (20). His method of analyzing the situation viewing himself and others as sovereigns is illustrated by his reasons for not telling Lucie of his desire for her love (39) and his long interior monologue trying to decide whether to go away with her immediately or wait until later, realizing that they will get together sooner or later, that "aucun engagement n'est définitif. Que tout affaire s'achève par un compromis. Que seule la mort, pour celui qui meurt, tranche absolument" (202).

Léone is, of course, the lion, described by Lucie: "Le lion est souverain. Comment ne le respecterait-on pas? Il peut croquer n'importe quelle autre bête; il a les plus grandes dents" (48). Léone, as Duc finally realizes, is the character Jeanne Treffort in his novel, whom he describes as "une belle femme . . . bien élevée . . . . Elle se conduisait bien . . . elle avait cet air d'aisance inimitable de ceux qui sont nés dans une famille fortunée" (117-18). She is the perfect wife and housekeeper because Duc thinks sweeping, dusting, and taking care of the house are the most intimate things in life and he wants her to be the one to do them. She is continually and unobstrusively cleaning the house, cooking meals, serving the others, and she always drops whatever she is doing to talk to Duc or go on an excursion with him. She even packs his suitcase when he leaves for his week-end with Lucie. The first thing she did upon going to Duc's apartment for the first time ten years earlier was to clean up the filth in which he lived, but, unlike Roberte, she respected Duc because he was "consciencieux dans son travail et dans l'expression de ce qu'il ressentait . . . honnête, d'abord avec lui-même" (109). At first the sight of greasy dishes made her sick, but she overcame this disgust and was proud of her victory over herself. Now she has learned how to do things with her hands and considers the housework as her work: "Je suis contente d'avoir, moi aussi, mon travail" (112).

She has sexual relations only with Duc, the game of love now seeming to her only a game and not one which she chooses to play. Duc, on the other hand, has relations with other women. Léone explains to Lucie that Duc hated women when she first met him because of the jealousy of his mother and two previous wives. It took her several years to convince him that she did not want to make of him her property. She now says that if he did not continue relations with other women, he would hate all women and even her. She prefers that Duc court Lucie rather than be in a bad mood because of not doing it, and she refuses to tell Duc of Lucie's humiliation because of his behavior: "Il m'apparenterait à sa mère et à ses précédentes épouses" (153).

Léone is characterized by equanimity although she frequently finds it in a tranquilizer called <u>équanil</u>. She is neither enthusiastic nor resigned at the games Duc plays with other drivers on the highway. She does gymnastic exercises regularly and relaxes on her chaise-longue with her feet higher than her head, "et les faux problèmes se révèlent ce qu'ils sont, c'est-à-dire problèmes qu'on a tort de se poser" (152). When Lucie asks her whether she, Duc, and Jean-Marie always know exactly what they want, she answers: "Non . . . . Mais nous essayons de bien nous tenir" (196). She is a civilized lion, one who has been "bien élevé" and who has continued the process by choice, a choice prompted by respect for Duc's work and his attitude toward it and himself.

According to Duc, he started "going toward" his métier after his rebirth following a cure for heroin addiction in 1942: "Il va à son métier, selon sa vocation qui est d'écrire en prose" (239). Like don Cesare, he was a few years earlier "comme mort"; don Cesare had been cured by seeing himself as outside himself and by seeing his own death. Duc made a list of his likes and dislikes, which he divided into chapters: "Il avait décidé de consacrer une journée (ou une semaine, ou un mois) de méditation, plume à la main, à chacun de ces chapitres. Cela devait faire un livre" (10). Even when "comme mort" he is a writer. In this case it is not the completion of the book which counts, but the writing as therapy, as a means of externalizing himself so he can better see himself. He did not finish the book, realizing one day that it did not interest him any longer. He sees this as the crisis which enabled him to pass from youth to maturity, to become interested in other matters besides politics, which was the cause of this crisis. He sees his life as a series of such crises. Don Cesare had built his life on a series of refusals leading to a narrowing of experience, a chipping away of the marble to make a statue; Duc sees his crises as an integral part of the growth process of the organism. The statue is also a result of natural and artistic metamorphoses and still bears the marks of those metamorphoses, but, although it may once have been molten, it was never alive. The plants which Duc raises "à contre-saison" are alive and:

> conservent, dans la forme de leur tige, de leurs feuilles, dans leur force ou leur chétivité, l'histoire des stades successifs de leur développement, histoire qui est, pour une part, celle de ses interventions, histoire qu'il leur a imposée, comme il s'est, pour une part, imposé à lui-même sa propre histoire. (165)

His novels are like the plants in that they show their own history including his interventions, but they also show his history and they influence it. Just as with the plant, the novelist is limited by the previous history and development of the genre and by the nature of present reality. After visiting the stonecutter's yard, a large family enterprise, Duc says that he wants to write the story of a great business enterprise as the growth and development of a plant, but that big business at present is not like this: "Laissons . . . les moyennes entreprises à leur nécessaire dépérissement. C'est un sujet pour romancier de la fin du XIXe siècle" (76). He is also limited by the nature of the particular novel on which he is working. Insisting that the characters do not exist before the novel, but that they are made as the novel is made, he uses as an example of diminishing chance an activity of the surrealist period, drawing lines on a blank sheet of paper:

> Mais de trait en trait la part du hasard dans le tracé du trait diminue . . . . Le premier trait était tracé au hasard absolument et le dernier ne pouvait être que ce qu'il était, aussi absolument que le premier avait pu être n'importe quoi. (32)

Duc faces the fact that after surrealism it is no longer possible to write invented stories as Balzac, Zola, Tolstoy, or Stendhal did.

Working with plants and writing a novel require hard work and a certain amount of self-discipline: "Pendant tout le temps qu'il écrivait un livre, il travaillait régulièrement, chaque après-midi, de trois à sept heures, et s'imposait, régime ou abstinence, ce qu'il estimait nécessaire pour se sentir dispos pendant les heures consacrées à l'écriture" (58). Part of Duc's weight is a reflection of the degree of control he has over himself and his moods; he says that at this particular time in his life, the quality of his writing depends on the state he is in, which in *325.000 francs* was called being *en forme*, and which Duc calls a state of grace and compares to:

> ce que les sportifs appellent la forme, les mystiques la grâce précisément, et les joueurs la chance. L'inverse: disgrâce, mauvaise forme ou malchance, pouvant se redresser, se renverser, se remettre au pas, par un changement de régime, une discipline plus stricte, ou davantage d'humilité devant la tâche à accomplir. (58-59)

The finished book is thus a record of his different states during the writing of the novel, and the book is composed like a season, "gelées blanches, sécheresses, pluies bienfaisantes, orages grêleux, chaleurs mûrissantes, dont l'alternance plus ou moins heureuse fait qu'elle est une bonne ou une mauvaise saison" (59). Duc himself is a living organism; what he says about love applies as well to writing or raising his plants:

> Pour Duc, qui s'estime tout un, qui refuse de se définir par ces abstractions: le corps, le coeur, l'esprit, l'âme et la mémoire, qui pense qu'à force de patience et d'expérience il s'est tout entier intégré à soi-même, chaque geste de l'amour, dans l'instant où il est accompli et s'il est exécuté avec bonheur, met en cause l'homme tout entier. (187)

The feeling of malaise he experiences in the first chapter is a total experience affecting even the landscape. The feeling is compared to swimming against the current, to feeling "gauche," and to dancing out of step (56). The disgrace shows up in all his endeavors; his car, extension of himself and symbol of his virility, is passed by a less powerful car; his plants are dying; and his novel is going badly.

The book he writes is a record to the world of his moods or state of grace, but it is also a way for him to understand himself, just as when he was "comme mort" or when playing a role in an imagined scenario he realizes that he is expressing his own desires: "Je ne parle plus de scénario, je parle de moi" (45). The novel he is trying to write is not in his usual manner because he wants to focus on a young, enthusiastic, and happy character:

> Enthousiaste n'est pas du tout un mot de son vocabulaire; mais, cette fois, et c'était vraiment nouveau pour lui, il avait envie de décrire l'enthousiasme. Son juvénile héros ne serait ni tué, ni emprisonné, ni humilié, ni trahi (ni châtré) comme il était arrivé à la plupart des jeunes hommes de ses précédents romans. (60-61)

He begins seeing his characters through the eyes of Lucie and realizes that he could never read parts of the novel to her. He analyzes the character of the _docteur_ and of the rich man in the scenario and wonders what disgrace they are hiding under "le masque d'un dieu tout-puissant" (85). He soon realizes that he is the one who is "frappé de disgrâce," but he continues the novel:

"C'était sa seule manière à lui, romancier, de faire la lumière en soi et de tirer la morale de l'affaire" (85). He wonders why he is so interested in these characters, why he has chosen the setting: "Il ne croyait pas au hasard en matière d'imagination" (92). His having chosen a seaport in Egypt as a setting leads him to remember his friend Kamal and his experiences in Egypt. This memory coupled with news of Kamal and events in Egypt at present lead to reflection and discussions with his friends, which in turn lead to a clearer understanding of himself and of his relation to the world. This process then becomes the object of the new novel. Writing the original novel and reacting with it lead him to the realization that he does not want to write about "l'amour fou," but to experience it, and that he does not want to write this novel, but another one.

The starting point for the idea of the _fête_ is: "Il n'y aurait pas de fêtes, s'il n'y avait pas de jours ouvrables" (48), a change of pace to keep step with the music, a time to do things one does not do ordinarily, or to provide relief from the regular schedule and thus restore a sense of pleasure to it. Duc, however, does not like what he calls a "fête châtrée," examples of which are listening to records, going to the theater or to movies, and visiting museums. He does all these things now, but formerly he could bear only "les spectacles dont j'étais en même temps l'acteur" (139). He explains that a _fête_ is an organic whole, which begins, develops, grows, and dies according to its own tempo and its own progression. He insists that Mark Antony did not have "la passion" for Cleopatra, but accompanied her because with her he was never bored. The sole purpose of their band of Commourants was to give each other _fêtes_, which is what he wants to do with Lucie. He wants a _fête_ of reciprocal love, which is the only kind a sovereign can permit himself, in its own place and its own time. For the _fête_ to succeed it must be entered into voluntarily by both parties, who accept to become object for the other, but also subject for the other object. To win Lucie's love, Duc must become once again like her, which is part of what the fête is all about, a respite from lucidity and sovereignty, a controlled experience of "amour fou," in which Diderot's "comédien" is himself and the character he is playing at the same time.

Since Lucie is an adolescent, he becomes a child: "Elle a l'impression qu'il la désire comme un enfant désire un jouet et qu'il tapera du pied si elle refuse, si elle se refuse. Cela devrait l'indigner. Mais au contraire elle est émue" (152). Kissing Lucie, Duc tries to forget everything he knows about kissing, thinking that he might offend her if he showed his expertise. In the fête d'amour each person becomes an object for himself in order to become object for the other, but he alternately accepts to be the subject acting on the other, "se remettre dans les mains de l'autre si absolument que la honte se change en orgueil et la douleur en plaisir" (189). During their lovemaking and walks in the park Lucie rids herself, with Duc's guidance, of false shame and learns to take pleasure as well as to give it. Then she drinks wine rather than fruit juices and wants to try foods she had disdained before, to overcome her former distastes. This is seen as a necessary step in the process of ceasing to be an adolescent and becoming an adult, a sovereign. The experience of alternating as subject and object is then transferred to the self, becoming subject and object for oneself, living one's own history and creating it at the same time. Rather than simply admiring the adolescent integrity as in previous novels, Duc recognizes that Lucie is ready to undergo a metamorphosis, recognizing it because he has undergone so many himself, and helps her to go through hers as she helps him to go through his.

His metamorphosis has to do with Duc as a novelist. The something new he wants to do in the novel is, taking Lucie as a pretext, to seize in its totality, without analyzing it, the singularity of Lucie, "ce qui la distingue absolument d'une autre, Lucie unique, et ce qu'il voudrait dire avec les mots justes" (78). Within the novel Duc is trying to see this singularity of Lucie. He realizes that it is almost impossible for him to see her as an object because his mood is affecting the way he sees her; what he sees as her "ton" is actually "son ton à lui, Duc, ces jours-ci" (126). The purpose of the photography session is to make of Lucie's face an object among objects: "L'objectif est un oeil qui voit mais qui ne perçoit pas" (179). Duc wants to find out all he can about Lucie, "de la dévoiler" (137). During their _fête_ he is able to do just that: "Duc continua de s'instruire de Lucie; il interrogeait son corps . . . durant les pauses, il continuait de lui poser des questions, précautionneusement, pour qu'elle se dévoilât sans panique, sans subterfuges" (261). Then on the afternoon he returns home from the _fête_, he opens a new notebook and jots down rapidly things she said, a particular expression of her face, and the transformations she underwent during the _fête_. The effort to find the "mot juste" puts an end to the inevitable sadness of separation, and he begins to feel "léger" (283).

Thus Duc is not a man "qui reste dans. Il est un homme qui va à" (246). His real "poids" is his "légèreté," his ability to change from the Duc in the beginning of the novel, who felt "lourd . . . enfermé dans ma souveraineté, comme si je traînais avec moi, accroché à mes hanches, un navire de haut bord" (100). Returning from the _fête_, he tells Léone that he knows where he is going; he will simply tell what happened during the preceding ten days. He considers himself lucky because his own life is a series of seasons, of novels, and he wonders why he previously had invented characters and imagined plots "alors qu'il n'avait qu'à faire l'inventaire de ses biographies juxtaposées" (284).

To Léone's assertion that he has always done this, he replies: "Plus de masque . . . plus d'affabulation. Nous allons serrer le vif" (284).

Duc is thus superior to don Cesare and also to Haroun Al-Rachid. Don Cesare looked at his life at the hour of his death and bore witness to himself of himself. Haroun Al-Richid had stories told to him by Scheherazade. Duc continues to have desires in life and proves himself by fulfilling them, by playing the roles necessary to fulfill them. In this case, he plans and executes a military campaign in which no one is actually hurt, he is the enthusiastic young man experiencing "l'amour fou," and he is the wise mentor helping an adolescent grow to maturity in a tender paternal, if not fraternal, relationship. Then he looks at himself and his experiences in a novel, which witnesses to himself and to readers what he was during the experience, what he weighed on the scale of reality. The completion or execution of that novel within the discipline of the métier is then another feat of prowess, weighing him on the scale of the professional. Such is _La Fête_, in which Duc is subject and object.

(the author himself in the novel is never quite sure whether she is or not), it seems obvious that La Truite is a trout and was so named by the author. A great part of the novel is the process by which this trout came into being, the relationship of the author to it, and a comparison between this relationship and that of other characters to the novel and to the real world.

Part I opens in a bowling alley in Paris in June 1960. The author, having finished bowling with a friend, is joined by other friends and acquaintances Saint-Genis, Mariline, and a married couple, Rambert and Lou. They are all fascinated by a young woman, Frédérique, who turns out to be an "arnaqueuse." In a classic hustle, she and her husband, Galuchat, win 800,000 francs from Saint-Genis and Rambert. The others go to a bar together, but Lou is miffed at Rambert, and the author does not care to go. He drops Lou off on his way home. In Part II the author six months later has occasion to visit the villa of Rambert and Lou in Monaco and finds Frédérique and Galuchat living with them. He begins to look at them as possible characters for a novel, and Rambert tells his version of the events in the intervening six months, including Frédérique's trip to California with Saint-Genis and Galuchat's suicide attempt. In Part III the author, upon his return to Paris, visits Saint-Genis, who tells his version of the events and what really happened in America. Three months later, in Part IV, the author has just begun La Truite and goes once more to Monaco and observes the deterioration of the situation. Frédérique tells him the story of her life and her marriage to the homosexual Galuchat, concluding with Rambert's plan to go away with her. Two weeks later Rambert appears at the author's apartment in Paris with the news that he had made arrangements to take care of Lou and Galuchat so Frédérique would be free to go away with him, but she and Galuchat have disappeared. Part V begins a year later when the author has completed the first four parts of La Truite and has just returned from an overseas trip of several months, undertaken after completing the writing. At Rambert's invitation he visits him and Lou in their new home, a dilapidated old factory where Rambert, with the help of a few workers, makes paper. The author observes their conditions, listens to their stories, and returns to Paris, where he, Saint-Genis, and Mariline discuss Frédérique and future possibilities of her relationship with the fabulously wealthy Isaac.

The author sees the bowling alley at the beginning of the novel as the inside of a whale, which is comforting like a womb; the pins are seen as the teeth of the monster, which grow back as soon as they have been broken. When one knows that Vailland at this time was an admiring reader of Henry Miller, it is difficult not to see in this description a statement of the position of the writer in relation to George Orwell's 1941 essay, "Inside the Whale," in which he compares the inside of the whale to a womb. Of Henry Miller, Orwell writes: "In his case the whale happens to be transparent. Only he feels no impulse to alter or control the process that he is undergoing. He has performed the essential Jonah act of allowing himself to be swallowed, remaining passive, *accepting*" (Orwell 18). He goes on to see the position of the writer at the time of the essay and for years to come as one of impotence in relation to changing society or having any effect on the structure of that society: "But from now onwards the all-important fact for the creative writer is going to be that this is not a writer's world. That does not mean that he cannot help to bring the new society into being, but he can take no part in the process *as a writer*" (23). His advice to writers is "Get inside the whale--or rather, admit you are inside the whale (for you *are*, of course). Give yourself over to the world process, stop fighting it or pretending that you control it; simply accept it, endure it, record it" (23-24).

The author of La Truite, watching the crowd in the bowling alley, but not hearing them because of the noise of the machinery, sees only their gestures and the movements of their mouths. He compares them to trout in a stagnant pond gasping for air. The size of the bowling balls is compared to the glass balls which hold fishnets on top of the water, corresponding to the image of the black veil toward the end of the novel. Those who have "le voile" make all kinds of gestures to get rid of it without realizing they have it, but each gesture "les précipite vers la mort" (224). Thus the action of the novel is placed between the womb and death; at the end of the first part of the novel the author makes clear that the name of the game is survival when he describes himself as someone who, after many experiences, knows "que la seule vraie force c'est de survivre et que c'est dérisoire" (49).

A few examples should suffice to illustrate the density of the novel. The name of the bowling alley is "Le Point du Jour." There actually is, or was in 1960, such a place; it and the other places and characters in the novel thus have a concrete existence in the real world outside the novel. Point du Jour is the title of a collection of André Breton's articles, published in 1934; there is thus the recognition of the part surrealism and Breton played in Vailland's personal and literary past and present, shown in the surrealistic, dream atmosphere of parts of La Truite. Au point du Jour is the French translation of one of Nietzsche's works dealing with morality, inviting the reader to compare and contrast the world of La Truite with the world as described by Nietzsche. The final words of La Truite, "Mais pour quoi faire?" (248), echo the same question near the end of Nietzsche's The Genealogy of Morals. The lack of any explicit response at the end of La Truite invites the reader to consider the applicability of Nietzsche's response to the situation in and of the novel. Another example of density is the black veil image, immmediately calling to mind "taking the veil," which Rambert does on two levels by turning to the church as a form of insurance "just in case," thereby, in the world of Vailland, separating himself from reality. The fact that Gobineau planned, but never wrote, a virulent attack on the society of his time to be entitled _Les Voiles noirs_ was certainly not unknown to Vailland. The same can be said for other connotations of the veil in the worlds of other writers who form a part of his heritage; the first one that comes to mind is Rousseau. Thus any discussion of the novel is not and cannot be exhaustive; _parole_ is itself and _langage_ at the same time, particularly in a work clearly intending to show this very fact.

The bowling alley is a symbol for the world outside the bowling alley; it is that world in microcosm, mechanistic and artificial with elaborate machinery which overpowers the individual. The machinery is invented and executed by man and is out of all proportion to the "jeu de quilles"; this machinery is compared in noise and complexity to a large locomotive and to the assembly lines of the Renault factories. Within the bowling alley there are only men and their machines. In a mechanistic society, it is the instruments which man has made which become the "natural" orders to which the animal world is compared, as in the description of the trout rising to the surface "comme une montgolfière qui s'élève dans le ciel" (67), with teeth which are "une scie à métaux," and attacking the other trout "avec un recul entre chaque coup de dent, comme la mitrailleuse entre chaque balle" (68). Similarly, it is not human excellence which is of value, but the excellence of machines and fabricated objects: "Nous avons mis en parallèle Mercedes et Cadillac, Jaguar et Alfa-Romeo, Peugeot et Citroen, comme font les hommes d'aujourd'hui quand ils trinquent, comme faisait Plutarque: Numa contre Lycurgue, Alexandre contre César" (92-93).

The pins in the bowling alley are compared to the female body and especially to prostitutes displaying themselves in the windows of bordellos in

Hamburg (12-13). The use of the game as sexual sublimation is reinforced by a remark made by Mariline about her youth when the boys called the girls "quilles": "Quand nous sortions de l'école, ils criaient 'à bas les quilles!' Ça voulait dire qu'ils avaient envie de nous tripoter, mais qu'ils n'osaient pas" (14). The elaborate machinery of the bowling alley is thus seen as a means whereby man tries to deal artificially with his biological nature, which is itself actually "second nature," that is, which has become a cultural manifestation rather than a natural drive to procreate. The world of the novel outside the bowling alley is filled with different ways of dealing with sex and different attitudes toward it, from the homosexual world of Galuchat to Rambert's desire to "have" a virgin as a status symbol. It is because of the predatory nature of the sex they see around them that Frédérique and her girlfriends form their secret society sworn "de ne jamais se laisser posséder par les garçons. C'étaient elles qui devaient posséder" (164). The author, whose aim is friendship and tenderness, admits that "avec une femme il faut bien commencer au lit, c'est une habitude dans les sociétés civilisées" (107).

The author sees bowling as an intellectual game making use of physical laws which can be known, but in which chance remains: "L'adresse corrige le hasard, mais le hasard demeure; c'est ce qui en fait, d'une manière analogue à la guerre, un jeu excitant pour l'esprit" (24). Like war, in the sense in which Duc spoke of it, bowling has its own rules and the rules governing how the game is played, it has a special dress and a special tone, that of the ritual. The players exhibit "dans les gestes, le maintien, sur le visage un air de connivence, comme s'ils participaient à un rite qu'il était interdit de dévoiler" (19). In addition to the secret society of bowlers and that of Frédérique and her girlfriends, there is also the club: "Le club, dans le langage de Saint-Genis (mais il dit aussi la coterie, le cercle, la société, la classe, le milieu), c'est là où se fait l'argent" (115). Even the ritual of bowling is sanctioned by money, although playing for money is strictly forbidden.

The largest and most important club in the novel is the American Paper and Boxes Company, an American business with a French branch of which Saint-Genis is director and for which Rambert works. All the important decisions are made at the home office in Los Angeles, a building which exemplifies the hierarchy of the company, a world of its own with its own jargon, its own structure, its own culture, which an outsider would not understand. Within the company itself, the greater the distance is from the top of the hierarchy, the greater is the ignorance of the decision-making process. Near the top, no one is ever sure of the power of anyone else, especially since the members of the top and intermediate echelons have interests of unknown quantity in other businesses. Rambert's ignorance of what goes on at these upper echelons inspires in him a superstitious, religious attitude toward the shadowy figures who move there, and he is convinced that in that rarefied atmosphere only justice reigns and petty personal feelings have no place. The author's comment is: "Les Grecs étaient moins respectueux de leur Olympe" (113).

It is in the context of this artificial, mechanistic, highly ritualized, civilized society that Frédérique makes her appearance in the bowling alley:

> Frédérique releva la tête et rit. Un rire sonore, clair, sans arrière-pensée. Le bowling s'éclaira. La baleine avait ouvert sa gueule et nous nous trouvions dans une prairie, au printemps, près d'un courant d'eaux vives dont la rumeur ne faisait qu'accompagner le rire de Frédérique. (32-33)

It is her freshness and her "inimitable style du lancer" which make her interesting to the author, prompting him to quote to himself the same poem by Baudelaire about the sterile woman quoted by Antoinette in Bon Pied Bon Oeil. He tells Mariline that Frédérique has everything which he loves "chez les femmes, chez les bêtes sauvages, chez les plantes, dans les fleuves; elle se développe avec indifférence" (22). His first reaction to her and Galuchat is a feeling of malaise because of their isolation in the midst of the crowd. He is struck by "le regard contradictoirement vif et noyé, comme pas tout à fait dégagé de l'animalité de l'enfance," by her state of "inachèvement, baby fat, dernières soies du cocon dont elle était en train de se dégager" (20). She thus is the last in a long line of "jeunes filles intègres" beginning with Annie in Drôle de Jeu, the unicorn being chased in dreams by Marat, Milan, and Duc. But unlike Beau Masque, who caught Pierrette Amable with such disastrous consequences, or Duc, who helped to civilize Lucie, the author tries not to have any effect on Frédérique because he is viewing her professionally. She is a further development of Mariette, a further regression to the state of savagery in a society where the young organism is not nurtured or educated, but allowed to react with its environment as best it can. The "integrity," the indifference are a function of her primitive nature, and the author states his personal preference for Mariline:

> Frédérique aussi rit, c'est un rire enfantin et cruel; Frédérique est inhumaine, elle date d'avant toute civilisation et c'est pour cela qu'elle nous fascine. Le rire de Mariline est tendre et inspire la tendresse; il n'est pas en deça, il est au-delà de l'expérience humaine. (234)

Although he records the present state of society and the kind of results it can expect to produce in the future, he personally opts for civilization, but civilization in contact with the natural world, with the processes of nature, civilization as seen in Clothilde "dans le val verdoyant, près d'Angoulême, se consacrant à l'éducation de ses enfants . . . s'occupant aussi, année par année, à défaire et refaire l'ordonnance du parc" (236), civilization as exemplified by a novel, by La Truite.

The world of the bowling alley, like any other, is a world of signs and codes. The novel is filled with acronyms which mean nothing to the uninitiated:

A.M.F (American Machine and Foundry Company), A.P.B.C. (American Paper and Boxes Company), A.A.P.B.C. (American and Asiatic Paper and Boxes Company), S.S.V.L. (Société Secrète des Vraies Luronnes), H.L.M., etc. There are all kinds of codes, like the "code de la route": "Je vis un grand P, lettre blanche sur fond bleu, je freinai, obliquai, stoppai" (233). The code which permeates the entire novel is, of course, language itself. There are numerous references to jargon, specialized vocabularies, regional accents and vocabularies. When Lou wants to give Rambert a tongue-lashing, she uses words she learned when they lived in a furnished apartment in the thirteenth arrondissement during the occupation (31). When Mariline calls Galuchat "un tordu," she and the author both laugh because "dans notre langage à Mariline et à moi, dix ans plus tôt, les tordus c'étaient les intellectuels qui n'arrivaient pas à prendre parti" (23). Just as vocabulary changes with time, so do the tone and style of language change according to personal reactions: "Son langage est généralement retenu. Mais il arrive que la présence de Lou déclenche chez lui une verve graveleuse" (30). Gestures, through use in society, become vocabulary: "Il leva le bras en direction de Lou et, de la main, en faisant claquer la phalange contre le pouce, lui fit signe de se taire, de la fermer" (31). Language and its use is only one component of the individuality of the person; all components identify that person. Lou's attire in the bowling alley--a black dress and mink stole--fit her vocabulary: "Encore une expression début de siècle. Lou vieillit mal" (31).

People engaged in the same kind of work have their own language; the stewardesses on the airplane joke with the steward "dans ce langage particulier aux gens de même profession et qui, aux autres, paraît codé" (121). As specialization increases, communication with those outside the "secret society" becomes increasingly difficult; Isaac's granddaughter and her husband can talk about their work with only a few other people scattered over the globe. Isaac at the age of seventy-eight began to study mathematics in an attempt to understand their work and to be able to communicate with them.

In La Loi man's triumph over nature was seen in using the wind to go against the wind. Now this same technique is used to take advantage of humanly-instituted codes, as seen when Saint-Genis discusses contracts over the long-distance telephone with a lawyer at his elbow. The author sees this as the height of man's conquest of nature, a lawyer at the service of a man who knows what he wants: "Reste à savoir ce qu'on veut et le prix qu'on est prêt à payer, problème de souverain, le seul digne du souverain" (126). In like manner the author writes La Truite with the Petit Larousse at his elbow (214), like any other writer. Unlike the work of some other writers, however, La Truite is intelligible, on one level or another, to anyone who can read the language and not only to the specialists and the initiated.

This is true because La Truite is not like the Palais Mimosa in Monaco, "building à usage commercial, siège de nombreuses sociétés fictives," where there is "un bureau d'orientation et d'information, dans un hall aux boîtes à lettres vides, sous dix étages de bureaux où aucun employé ne travaille" (60), where "le signe, le sigle s'y est substitué à toute réalité" (61). The results of living in this kind of world can be seen in the description of Rambert's secretaries, who have lost "tout éclat, toute fraîcheur" (62). The same thing happens to animals when they live in an artificial situation, as seen in the trout who have lived in the pond too long and have settled into a rigid hierarchy, accustomed to resignation and submission. Frédérique, who grew up raising trout to be sold for food, knows that this kind of life decreases their value: "Truite lâche: viande puante" (70). La Truite is not, like the Palais Mimosa, an empty façade, but contains real people in a real world as seen by Roger Vailland.

The novel may be, among other things, a game, but this novel clearly shows that in games, as in everything else, there are degrees of artificiality. The game of bowling against an opponent is thus seen as less artificial than the way Lou and Rambert keep score in the afternoons when Rambert comes to practice; he bowls against himself, Rambert 1 against Rambert 2, and Lou waits until the end of the match to decide, depending on her mood, whether he is really the winner or the loser. This game at least has some value because he is getting practice to become better able to participate in a "real" game, whereas Lou's playing the slot machine is even more artificial. She plays the penny machine trying to make all three "signs" agree; it is a game over which she has no control played on a machine she knows has been rigged by the owner of the bar. But she continues to play: "Lou, aussi avide des 7500 francs du spot que des 3.500.000 francs du numéro plein à la roulette; pour le vrai vorace, bouffeur de signes, la valeur du signe n'a pas d'importance" (64).

The most important sign in the world of the novel is money, and the market value of a thing or of a person is the most important value. "Le standing," prestige, self-esteem are measured in the objects one owns or the price one is willing to pay for an object, and everyone is assumed to be an object for sale one way or another. Saint-Genis sees Frédérique and other members of the "club" as stocks: "En les arnaquant au bowling . . . Frédérique a acquis le droit d'être cotée à leur bourse; elle a acquis un titre, elle est devenue un titre" (115-16). Money and stocks circulate; when Frédérique has to leave California because of Galuchat's suicide attempt, Saint-Genis wonders whether he should give her some money to put her back in circulation (148).

Saint-Genis is an example of légèreté in relation to money, while still remaining in the "club." He always knows how much money he can let go for pleasure, for business, or for any other reason. He is not possessed by money, but sees in it "un divertissement," taking delight in figuring out the mechanisms which make money "work" in the same way he used to figure out how the gears on his bicycle worked when he was a boy. He also has a taste for absurd situations, always interested in seeing how he will comport himself in them, what profit or pleasure he can gain from them, and what new way of looking at things he may discover. But he is easily bored when his curiosity is not awakened. He actually has no money: "Il fait des opérations, il entre dans des combinaisons, mais il ne dispose d'aucun capital. Il gagne sa vie. Il fait son petit business, en prenant le temps de vivre" (238). The author is very much like Saint-Genis in his attitude toward life and toward money, stating to Rambert that he never saves money. He also has his little business, writing, and he writes about a variety of topics, showing that he has many interests.

The futility of having money for its own sake or of trying to use it as nourishment in a natural process is seen in the figure of Isaac, who is so wealthy he is beyond money. Like don Cesare, he has nothing but scorn for his relatives who love money: "Le seul péché contre l'esprit, disait-il, c'est de confondre le signe avec le concret, le singulier, d'aimer le signe, de se nourrir du signe; l'argent est un signe" (150). Money cannot buy him the one thing he really wants, the ability to communicate with his granddaughter. He has nothing to leave to her because he does not believe in the existence of any "placements sûrs" and is convinced that any portfolio not managed by a professional rapidly deteriorates. What Isaac has, what makes him powerful, is himself, "sa connaissance des hommes . . . et son entraînement à l'algèbre des affaires, sa capacité de jouer avec des abstractions . . . . Cela ne se lègue pas" (150). Isaac believes in the necessary destruction of any speculative fortune which ceases to be governed by the one who created it "par le seul jeu de son intelligence" (245). What the author has created by the play of his intelligence, but not by that alone, remains to be consumed by present readers and future generations.

Lou and Rambert are the two in the novel who have "le voile," who have given up the relationship to any reality outside themselves and their struggle with each other. With the aid of time and Frédérique, they end up imprisoned in a classic love-hate, mother-child relationship, which is linked specifically to Christianity: "Nous étions comme la foule le long du chemin de croix: 'et Lou tomba pour la première fois'; on a beau connaître le dénouement nécessaire de la Passion, c'est un beau spectacle qu'on a toujours envie de voir jusqu'au bout" (34). Lou is a strong woman who has fallen victim to "la passion," who has tried to make of another person the image of herself or an image she has created, and who is now possessed by that person. Trying to create another human being, however, is not as artificial as what Lou finally settles for; the author thinks that the day Lou began to have the "voile" was the day she began accepting diamonds from Rambert in exchange for allowing him to spend weekends with other women. The characters the author "creates" in the novel are not projections of his imagination, but people and things he actually observes, specifically situated in a "real" time and place.

Rambert, according to Frédérique, "ne fait pas le poids" (210). He is, in his relation to life, the antithesis of the author in relation to life and to his novel. Rambert also represents those parts of the author as author which he is shedding by writing this novel. Rambert's actions are usually prompted by negative motives; Saint-Genis maintains that Rambert chases women, not because of any love for them or for the chase, but rather as a gesture against Lou. Any chasing the author does is part of a creative process. Rambert is devious and deceitful: "C'est dans sa nature d'édifier à propos de n'importe quoi tout un système de mensonges" (107), while the author creates a fictional system based on observation of concrete reality. Rambert is possessed by hatred, which leads to a desire to possess others; the author is emotionally detached from his characters and is interested in them only as they pertain to the novel. The antithesis of Rambert's superstitious nature is seen throughout the novel in the author's interest in how things work and his refusal to consider anything as sacred.

Rambert's "métier" is taking over bankrupt paper mills and putting them on a sound footing, then selling them for a profit; this is analogous to what the author does when he observes a "bankrupt" society, orders it in his mind and in a novel, and then sells it, perhaps changing the society and perhaps not. At the time the novel begins, Rambert has put all his profits into land speculation in Monaco, using borrowed money to carry on the paper-mill business. The author says that Rambert has had "le voile" since he gave up fabrication for speculation. He does have a hobby in which he fabricates objects; one of his passions is woodworking, for which he has a variety of expensive machinery and receives catalogues from all over the world so he can order new gadgets and tools. The object which he and Galuchat are making when the author visits them is "une table d'accouchée du début du règne de Louis XV, au tiers de la taille du modèle" (54). Here, as in bowling, his forte is technique, but the object which he fabricates is a less-than-life-sized copy of an object which someone else made in the past; it has nothing to do with himself and the present, just as his study is a copy of an English style which he liked during a past period of his life (162). Rambert recognizes the efficacy of this kind of work as therapy for Galuchat's "dépression nerveuse" because it is precise manual work which occupies the hand and the mind; but it is not creative.

The American Indians on the reservation visited by Frédérique and Saint-Genis also make copies of objects created by a past culture, "des étoffes tissées et brodées à la main, des coiffures de plumes, des cuirs incrustés, des calumets, quantité d'objets fabriqués sur place, sous la direction d'ethnologues qui veillent à ce que les Indiens ne s'écartent pas des traditions de leur artisanat" (138). These objects differ among themselves, but they are all more "valuable" than the objects made by Rambert because they are bought and sold, some to be used up or consumed and some to be exhibited as pseudo-art objects, but they will all enter into circulation. They are probably more "valuable" than the shoes Frédérique buys in Los Angeles which, because they are made by hand in the Basque countries and imported into America, are more "valuable" than shoes made in America, but less "valuable" than the Indian crafts because they are intended entirely for consumption. The novel as written by the author is an object made by hand, by a man rather than by a machine, an object which is also an art object intended to be sold to circulate in order to be consumed.

The art objects most prominent in the novel are paintings. Mariline prior to the time of the novel sold paintings on commission, but in the novel she buys only for herself from the artists, who are all old friends of hers. These paintings do not actually enter into circulation. In like manner, the gallery where Galuchat worked, "une boutique comme ces années-là les industriels en achetaient à leurs femmes pour qu'elles s'occupent l'après-midi," was bought for him by his homosexual lover, his "tuteur." The business in the gallery consisted of buying from friends of the tutor in order to sell to other friends; all the paintings are "sans valeur marchande, peintes par les amis des amis du tuteur et abandonnées là" (199). Other paintings in the novel are bought by companies like the A.P.B.C. to decorate their office buildings and to give them "prestige," but also as a tax deduction.

Other status-symbol objects prominent in the novel are expensive cars, mink coats, and Dior gowns. Another kind of status symbol is the trophy, the scalp, the visible proof of an exploit or of a "possession." On the Indian reservation the Indians consent to photographs for set prices depending on the kind of photograph, but if the tourists can catch them off guard, it does not cost anything. The white men end up stalking the Indians trying to get a picture, not so much to avoid paying as to "saisir le cheval et l'Indien dans leur mouvement naturel" (138). They have, of course, all kinds of expensive equipment with which to do this. On the other hand, Verjon, a friend of Frédérique's father, has the actual "scalps" of the fish he has caught and keeps them in a room called the "museum," each stuffed specimen with its label giving all the particulars of the catch. The fragility of this kind of collection is shown by Frédérique's throwing the trophies of a lifetime into the lake. Similarly Rambert actually throws away, hoping to "get" Frédérique, "le produit de la vente de ses terrains et immeubles de Monaco, toute sa fortune, les économies de vingt ans, dix-huit papeteries déficitaires remises sur pied" (209).

La Truite is different from all these other objects. In the first place, the novel as written by the author is not fabricated, but created, making use of the natural processes in a manner analogous to that used to raise trout in the hatchery. The trout are fed meat from a slaughterhouse which is not in the same place as the hatchery; in like manner, the "meat" of the novel, the content, does not come from the place where the writing occurs. The fish are fed meat from sick cows because this is cheaper and, according to Frédérique, fish cannot catch the illnesses of cattle; La Truite can feed on sick characters and a sick society and still be a healthy novel. Just as the writer must be "en forme" to write, Frédérique does a few exercises and takes deep breaths before beginning the delicate process of making the female drop the eggs:

> La truite se débattait. Frédérique la laissait s'apaiser. C'est le plus difficile. Il faut une main ferme et douce et une certaine familiarité avec les truites, qui ne s'acquiert pas; il faut que l'animal se sente en confiance et, bien qu'il étouffe, n'attende pas de la main un surcroît de souffrance (et d'angoisse), mais une délivrance, qu'il se laisse aller à la main, dans la main. (181-82)

When the author says of Frédérique: "Je la tenais. Il était temps" (164), it is obvious that this cry is not analogous to that of Verjon with his catch, of Rambert with his prey, or of the tourists skulking in the bushes, but rather of Frédérique during the fertilization process. The author thus describes his behavior with her: "Nous n'avons presque rien bu: je tenais à garder le contrôle de sa confession et surtout de mes questions; il devait être facile de la heurter, qu'elle se bute. . . . Heureusement que je connais bien les petites filles de province" (164). On another occasion he writes: "Je cherche des périphrases; j'ai encore peur de la brusquer, qu'elle se referme" (184). Just as Frédérique must devote much time and patience to collecting the eggs from the females, but has no trouble collecting the sperm from the males, so the author in collecting the stories of Rambert and Saint-Genis simply asks a prudent question from time to time or prods the memory gently. Frédérique uses "une plume" to mix the eggs and the sperm: "C'est un autre moment délicat de la fécondation et qui exige une main sûre et un certain don" (182). As with <u>La Truite</u>, whether the eggs have been fertilized or not is not known until later when the eyes appear or do not appear "sous la coque translucide" (182-83).

So <u>La Truite</u> is a fabricated object which circulates, but it is also a living organism produced in a controlled, laboratory situation by someone who knows what he is doing, by someone who is a professional. Of Lou, Rambert, Frédérique, and Galuchat the author writes: "Je commençais de les envisager sous l'angle du professionnel" (79). He thus is also a member of society, belonging to one of its professional groups with its duties, prerogatives, and aims. Visiting Rambert's villa for the first time, he is disgusted by the behavior of Lou and Rambert and wants to leave slamming the door behind him, but he remains because "un romancier a des devoirs. . . . Il était possible que Lou, Frédérique, Rambert et Galuchat fussent des personnages pour moi" (79). One of his duties is to be precise and describe as scientifically as possible what he observes; describing what happens to Rambert's face in moments of violent emotion, he writes: ". . . et l'homme véritable apparaît, véritable je n'en sais rien, un autre homme en tout cas" (86). He has a specific relation to his characters and is dealing with them for the purpose of describing them in a novel. When Frédérique cannot remember the names of the different ranks in her secret society, he writes: "Un psychiatre aurait insisté pour qu'elle trouve les termes; mais je ne faisais pas de thérapeutique, je me renseignais sur mon personnage; je n'insistai donc pas" (167). He has a duty to the reader; he specifies that her recital was not just as he transcribes it: "Je la laissais aller et puis je revenais en arrière, pour 'boucher les trous'" (173).

The author is not the flic-confesseur which Rambert shows himself to be when he relates how he felt when Galuchat told him his story. Rambert felt for Galuchat in that moment a kind of sadistic "tendresse." The author is not emotionally involved in the fate of his characters; when Rambert insists that the author dislikes him and wants to see him defeated, the author answers: "Je ne t'aime pas. Mais je me fous que tu te casses la gueule ou pas" (93). His is the clinical detachment of an ethnologist; asking Frédérique about Isaac: "Je l'interroge prudemment, ne voulant pas la mettre en éveil sur la richesse d'Isaac (ne voulant pas intervenir dans le vie de mon personnage, provoquer des réactions qui ne seraient pas dans sa manière)" (204). His relationship with Saint-Genis is different in that the latter is a friend and also a character. As Saint-Genis tells his story, the author questions him on his feelings at the time. Saint-Genis says he never analyzes his feelings, but he tries and concedes that the author was right to question him because he had forgotten that first evening.

As a professional and as a human being, the author also has a personal duty to himself and to his friends; he lets the reader know that he cannot tell some of the most beautiful actions in which he has participated or of which he has personal knowledge because they involve friends who are still living or parts of himself from which he is not yet "detached": "Je ne peux pas écorcher vifs mes amis et moi-même pour le plaisir d'écrire. Si je leur survis--à eux et à moi--j'aurai des histoires tout à fait extraordinaires à raconter" (159). So the professional does not "scalp" himself and his friends so as to have something to write about, but instead writes a novel in which he appears with scalp intact: "La peau . . . mon reflet dans le monde et le reflet du monde en moi, lieu où la réalité devient reflet et le reflet réalité . . ." (80).

La Truite, it must not be forgotten, is also a living organism. The author explains to the reader his behavior on his second visit to Monaco, saying that this is the first time he has attempted to write a story without knowing the ending. He hopes it will have an ending because, if not, he might be tempted to invent one. He would not like to do this because "la vérité de la vie est presque toujours plus _forte_ que la vérité romanesque" (158). He continues by saying that life, which he calls "l'histoire" of a society or of an individual, is usually organized into actions which begin and end; a novelist tells "des histoires": "Une bonne histoire est bien organisée (comme un organisme vigoureux)" (158). The reason he did not begin writing this novel earlier is that he is interested only in tragedy, which, inspired by Racine, he defines as involving only the action of "souverains" (159). The first night in the bowling alley, it seemed possible an action was beginning, but the people involved were not sovereigns, with the possible exception of Frédérique. With his professional standards, he was not interested in that action. However, the story of Saint-Genis, ending with Frédérique leaving California seated on the plane beside Isaac, interested him because Isaac and the other tamanoirs at the top of the hierarchy "sont les souverains du monde contemporain (à l'Occident), souveraineté abstraite" (159).

One reason Frédérique is so successful with trout is the affinity of animal for animal. In the same way, it is evident that the author and La Truite are animals: "Un vrai animal . . . sait se servir non seulement des hommes et des choses mais aussi des idées, comme l'animal se sert de ce qu'il mange, boit, respire pour se faire son plumage, son poil, ses griffes, ses crocs . . ." (195). He makes a comparison between himself when he writes and Frédérique; she goes her way, taking what she needs to accomplish something she has not formulated, in the same way he says he writes: "Les jours de bonne forme, je ne sais pas où ma phrase, mon récit me mènent, mais je vais à coup sûr. Quand je suis en train d'écrire un roman, je ne remarque dans la vie que ce qui servira au roman" (206). As examples of the fact that for animals and for artists "la réalisation précède et révèle le projet," he uses a hare following the path of another hare and suddenly jumping to the top of a wall and watching the hounds in pursuit of his "fantôme"; or Velasquez, thinking he is painting the surrender of Breda, but actually creating "un pelage sombre troué de soleil, la fourrure fastueuse d'une bête plus vraie que nature" (133).

Frédérique, and by extension the author and the novel, is "plus animal qu'un vrai animal . . . . Elle procède comme l'imagination. Comme les bêtes se construisent, se développent, muent ou se métamorphosent, en imaginant et en s'imaginant" (195). Saint-Genis says she moves in a dark world with no premeditation and no conscious aim, like the "larve qui se fait matériau pour construire son imago, l'image resplendissante d'elle-même qu'elle découvrira en se découvrant. Elle précède comme un rêve réel" (151).

Technically this is done the way Saint-Genis reflects, by juxtaposition and superposition of images "jusqu'à ce que leur assemblage lui paraisse cohérent, nécessaire, que ça 'tienne debout,' . . . que ça ne puisse plus être autrement, comme la vie dans le moment où on la vit" (25). So the author's final words referring to Frédérique also refer to *La Truite*: "Qu'elle tienne, bon dieu, qu'elle tienne" (247). If it does hold together, it is itself and the material of which it is made, the food with which it has been nourished, the western world in 1960 and 1961 and Roger Vailland as he reacts with it. The reader can then say of *La Truite* what Vailland writes of Frédérique, in a rather lengthy "poème":

> Je commence à la saisir dans sa singularité. Comme un chêne dont on sait d'abord qu'il est un arbre plus dur que le châtaignier, moins parfumé que le merisier, un modèle éventuel pour un peintre figuratif, qu'il est généreux, que son feuillage est un poumon vif et dix mille oiseaux le picorent, que chacune de ses branches recherche si douleureusement la lumière qu'elle en est percluse, qu'il a cinq cents ans, qu'il a vu passer Louis XIV et sa meute lancés à la poursuite d'un loup et que le chemin qui le contourne mène à un taillis de hêtres où nous trouverons des *trompettes de mort*, qu'il est beau, qu'il est laid et vient le jour où il est enfin ce chêne-là, à cet endroit-là, à ce moment-là. (207-208)

An *explication de textes* of this poem would reveal in the imagery, in the movement, and in the whole, what is essentially "Vailland." The distance traveled from Marat enclosed in his rational subjectivity viewing the tree as different objects depending on the perspectives is clearly intended to show the Vailland who is part of _La Truite_ and part of the world of _La Truite_. In this world he compartmentalizes his life as Marat did, performing as a professional and thus living his historical time, but reserving his personal life, thereby also living his historical time which makes that reservation necessary. Within the novel his "self-in-the-world" is seen in operation. In the real world _La Truite_ is this "self-in-the-world," circulating to nourish others--economically, intellectually, and artistically--and at the same time, during Vailland's lifetime, making money to nourish Vailland so he might perhaps create another animal, which would contain the image of the Vailland who resulted from feeding on _La Truite_.

CONCLUSION

Jean-Jacques Brochier sees the life and work of Roger Vailland as a kind of Bildungsroman (Brochier 11), and it is certainly a fact that there are few writers who have left such a novelistic record of continuing reciprocal influence of life and novel. In the 1945 essay quoted in the introduction, Vailland made clear the importance for him of free, pleasurable action, which he saw at that time as the domain of the amateur rather than of the professional. In other essays he continued to explore the meanings of freedom, pleasure, and action, using the genre which allows the writer the freedom to say what he thinks to be true or wishes to be true, the freedom to form an hypothesis, the freedom to be an amateur. But for Vailland there is no freedom and no pleasure without action in the real world. The novels thus become the necessary testing ground for the ideas, a world seen as the "real" world as opposed to the intellectual, abstract world of the essay. It is obvious that Vailland used each novel to test his ideas and to judge past or future life-styles; each novel is a means of looking at himself and the world and the relations between them.

Vailland and many of his characters, especially Marat in Drôle de Jeu and Duc in La Fête, saw their lives as a series of discontinuous seasons which, once ended, were recorded in a novel. As he realized and made clear in La Fête and in La Truite, the novels are not simply the record of a season, but are an integral part of the season, the necessary link between the seasons. Each completed novel contains within itself its own antithesis, and the Vailland at the end of the novel is not the Vailland who began writing the novel. Each novel necessitates a new novel to resolve the conflicts made apparent in the previous one. Each resolution is seen as too extreme, necessitating another look in order to *faire le poids*, to balance the extreme position, to restore a lost equilibrium which actually never existed. In addition, just as he was changing by reacting with the novel in progress and the world of that novel, the real world with which he was reacting was also changing.

The problem, as he soon realized, lay in trying to use language to define lucidly and rationally a complex living organism--himself--and its environment, conditioning and nourishing each other. In *La Truite*, he succeeded in demonstrating this process of continuous action, reaction, and interaction, the creation which is never *ex nihilo*, but is what it is at a given moment, the result of many past influences, and more or less useful as part of a new creation. Within the novels the problem of acting in the world while leaving others as free as possible to act, and being left free by them, is solved (not definitively) by playing the role of the professional, by observing and describing. Any teaching or nourishing does not take place on a personal livel within the novel, but is accomplished by the work, the self in the world, which thus becomes the "real" self, the self capable of action in the world. Playing with words was always a pleasure for Vailland; acceptance of this play as a profession is also an acceptance of the system with its limitations and its possibilities. Playing with words thus becomes a paradigm of the human condition, and the creation of an identifiable "Vailland" describing Vailland and his environment is a triumph of human freedom.

Thus the *Bildungsroman* has a very neat ending, but only because Vailland died without being able to live the next season and write the next novel to balance this extreme. The nature of *La Truite*, with its sharp teeth attacking like a machine gun, announces the novel which was not written, as does

Vailland's last published article, which appeared in _Le Nouvel Observateur_ for November 26, 1964. In this article, entitled "Éloge de la Politique," he wrote:

> Se conduire en politique, c'est agir au lieu d'être agi, c'est faire l'histoire, faire la politique au lieu d'être fait, d'être _refait par elle_. . . . Comme citoyen, je veux qu'on me parle politique, je veux retrouver, je veux provoquer l'occasion de mener des actions politiques (des vraies), je veux que nous redevenions tous des politiques. (_Oeuvres Complètes_ X 440,445)

Roger Vailland was not able to survive into this new season or to write the novel of May 1968, which would have been written by Vailland the professional novelist, but no one knows what the Vailland in the novel might have been.

WORKS CITED

Brochier, Jean-Jacques. *Roger Vailland, tentative de description*. Paris: Eric Losfeld, 1969.

Gobineau, Comte de. *Les Pléïades*. Paris: Librairie Générale Française, 1960.

Orwell, George. "Inside the Whale." *Henry Miller: Three Decades of Criticism*. Ed. M. Mitchell. New York: New York Univ.Press, 1971. 7-25.

Vailland, Roger. "De l'Amateur." 1951. *Le Regard Froid*. 111-132.

---. *Beau Masque*. Paris: Gallimard, 1954. (Folio).

---. *Bon Pied Bon Oeil*. Paris: Buchet-Chastel, 1950. (Livre de Poche).

---. *Drôle de Jeu*. Paris: Buchet-Chastel, 1945. (Livre de Poche).

---. *Écrits Intimes*. Paris: Gallimard, 1968.

---. "Éloge de la Politique." *Le Nouvel Observateur* 26 Nov. 1964. Rpt. in *Oeuvres complètes* 10: 437-45.

---. *La Fête*. Paris: Gallimard, 1960. (Collection Soleil).

---. *Un Jeune Homme Seul*. Paris: Corrêa, 1951.

---. *La Loi*. Paris: Gallimard, 1957. (Livre de Poche).

---. *Les Mauvais Coups*. Paris: Éditions du Saggitaire, 1949.

---. "Le Procès de Pierre Soulages." 1962. *Le Regard Froid* 133-139.

---. "Quelques Réflexions sur la singularité d'être français." 1945. *Le Regard Froid* 9-30.

---. *Oeuvres complètes*. Ed. Jean Recanati. 10 vols. Lausanne: Éditions Rencontre, 1968.

---. *Le Regard Froid*. Paris: Bernard Grasset, 1963.

---. *325.000 francs*. Paris: Buchet-Chastel, 1955. (Livre de Poche).

---. *La Truite*. Paris: Gallimard, 1964. (Collection Soleil).

PRIMARY WORKS CONSULTED

---. "Artur Rimbaud ou Guerre à l'homme." *Le Grand Jeu* 2 (1929). Rpt. in *Cahiers de l'Herne* 10 (1968): 96-100.

---. "Avant les Vingt-quatre Heures du Mans." *France-Soir* June 1957. Rpt. in *Oeuvres complètes* 10: 385-425.

---. *Batailles pour l'Humanité*. Vélodrome d'Hiver, Paris. 21 April 1954. *Oeuvres complètes* 5: 217-254.

---. "La Bestialité de Montherlant." *Le Grand Jeu* 1 (1928). Rpt. in *Cahiers de l'Herne* 10 (1968): 72-73.

---. *Boroboudour, Voyage à Bali, Java et autres îles*. 1951. *Oeuvres complètes* 6: 11-182.

---. "Le Carnet de comptes d'un homme heureux." 1957. *Le Regard Froid* 141-68.

---. "Choix d'articles." *Roger Vailland, Deux Études*. Ed. René Ballet and Elisabeth Vailland. Paris: Éditions Pierre Seghers, 1973. 60-186.

---. *Choses Vues en Égypte*. 1952. Rpt. in *Oeuvres complètes* 6: 185-300.

---. *Chronique des années folles à la libération*. Ed. René Ballet. Paris: Messidor/Éditions sociales, 1984.

---. "Sur la Clôture, la règle et la discipline." 1958. *Le Regard Froid* 243-49.

---. *Le Colonel Foster plaidera coupable*. Paris: Grasset, 1973.

---. "Colonisation." Le Grand Jeu 1 (1928). Rpt. in Cahiers de l'Herne 10 (1968): 77-78.
---. "Défense de l'amateur." Nouvelles littéraires 5 Dec. 1957: 1, 8.
---. "La Dernière Bataille de l'armée de Lattre." 1945. Rpt. in Oeuvres complètes 10: 283-314.
---. "Écrits politiques." 1945-47. Rpt. in Oeuvres complètes 10: 315-16.
---. "Eichmann et ses juges." France-Observateur April 1961. Rpt. in Oeuvres complètes 10: 337-53.
---. "Éloge du cardinal de Bernis." 1956. Le Regard Froid 169-241.
---. "Entretien; Roger Vailland: Mes Amis sont au chômage." Interview with Madeleine Chapsal. L'Express 29 April 1964: 31-32.
---. "Les Entretiens de madame Merveille avec Octave, Lucrèce et Zéphyr." 1946. Le Regard Froid 45-70.
---. "Esquisse pour un portrait du vrai libertin." 1946. Le Regard Froid 31-43.
---. Expérience du drame. Paris: Corrêa, 1953. Rpt. in Oeuvres complètes 5: 115-215.
---. "La Guerre au jour le jour." 1944-45. Rpt. in Oeuvres complètes 10: 189-280.
---. Héloïse et Abélard. Paris: Corrêa, 1947.
---, with Raymond Manevy. Un Homme du peuple sous la Révolution. 1936. Rpt. in Oeuvres complètes 10: 9-188. Rpt. Paris: Gallimard, 1979.
---. Interview. Le Nouvel Observateur 25 Feb. 1965: 27.
---. Laclos par lui-même. Paris: Éditions du Seuil, 1953.
---. "Jenny Merveille." Livres de France Dec. 1959: 7-9.
---. "Léopold III devant la conscience belge." 1945. Rpt. in Oeuvres complètes 10: 357-82.
---. Lettres à sa famille. Ed. Max Chaleil. Paris: Gallimard, 1972.
---. Les Liaisons dangereuses 1960. Film adaptation with Roger Vadim. Paris: Julliard, 1960. Rpt. in Oeuvres complètes 5: 255-357.
---. "Lisez Flaubert." France-Observateur 7 Sept. 1960. Rpt. in Oeuvres complètes 10: 427-35.
---. "Sur Manon Lescaut." 1967. Rpt. in Oeuvres complètes 9: 299-312.
---. Monsieur Jean. Paris: Gallimard, 1959. Rpt. in Oeuvres complètes 5: 7-113.
---. "L'Oeuvre de cruauté, suivi de La distraction de soi d'avec soi comme source du sublime." 1950. Le Regard Froid 89-108.
---. "Les Quatre Figures du libertinage." 1950. Le Regard Froid 71-87.
---. "Le Retour à la sauvagerie." Interview with S. Woods. Le Nouvel Observateur 13 May 1965: 16-18.
---. La Réunion. 1964. Rpt. in Oeuvres complètes 6: 301-407.
---. "Roger Vailland répond au questionnaire Marcel Proust." Livres de France Dec. 1959: 6.
---. "Suétone: Les Douze Césars." 1962. Rpt. in Oeuvres complètes 9: 169-298.
---. Le Surréalisme contre la Révolution. Paris: Éditions Sociales, 1948.

OTHER WORKS CONSULTED

Abraham, Pierre. "Faire la Loi." Europe 34.144 (Dec. 1957): 140-44.

Adam, George. "Roger Vailland à l'heure du Prix." Figaro littéraire Dec 1957: 1,4.

Albérès, R. M. "Profession: Amateur." Nouvelles littéraires 21 March 1968: 5.

Aragon, Louis and André Breton. "À suivre--Petite contribution au dossier de certains intellectuels à tendances révolutionnaires." Variétés June 1929.

d'Aubarède, Gabriel. "Rencontre avec Roger Vailland." Nouvelles Littéraires 5 Dec. 1957: 8.

Ballet, René and Elisabeth Vailland. Roger Vailland, Deux études. Écrivains d'hier et d'aujourd'hui 43. Paris: Éditions Pierre Seghers, 1973.

Boisdeffre, Pierre de. "Un Laclos marxiste: Roger Vailland." Une Histoire vivante de la littérature d'aujourd'hui. Paris: Le Livre Contemporain, 1959. 290-94.

---. "Roger Vaillant [sic] en quête d'une éthique." Où va le roman? Paris: del Duca, 1962. 158-63.

Bott, François. Les Saisons de Roger Vailland. Paris: Grasset, 1969.

Bourdet, Denise. "Roger Vailland." Revue de Paris 65 (April 1958): 128-32.

Bourin, André. "Esquisse pour un portrait." Livres de France Dec. 1959: 4-5.

Brasillach, Robert. Notre Avant-guerre. Paris: Plon, 1941.

Brisville, Jean-Claude. "Le Petit Duc." Preuves 117 (Nov. 1960): 84-86.

Brochier, Jean-Jacques. "Les Romans de Roger Vailland." Magazine littéraire 8 (June 1967): 18-22.

Buchet, Edmond. Les Auteurs de ma vie ou ma vie d'éditeur. Paris: Buchet-Chastel, 1969.

Caillet, Gérard. "Roger Vailland." Hommes et Mondes 63 (Oct. 1951): 127-18.

Caute, David. Communism and the French Intellectuals, 1914-1960. New York: Macmillan, 1964.

Chaleil, Max, ed. Entretiens: Roger Vailland. Rodez: Éditions Subervie, 1970.

Chapsal, Madeleine. "Roger Vailland." Les Écrivains en personne. Paris: Julliard, 1960. 235-51.

Charmatz, Jacques. "Le Roman idéologique dans l'oeuvre romanesque de Roger Vailland." Littérature et idéologies. La Nouvelle critique spécial 39 bis (1970): 266-270.

Chiaromonte, Nicola. "Letter from Paris: Gide, Sartre and Cafe Communism." New Republic 124 (7 May 1951): 16-18.

Choublier, Claude. "Roger Vadim et Roger Vailland révèlent comment a été conçue et réalisée l'adaptation des Liaisons dangereuses." La Nef 16.31 (Oct. 1959): 71-80.

Decaunes, Luc. "Les Mauvais Coups." Paru 51 (Feb.-March 1949): 21-24.

Dort, Bernard. "Épreuves du roman, des travaux et des jours." Cahiers du Sud 41.328 (April 1955): 467-74.

Dubois, Claude. "Vailland contre Céline." La Quinzaine littéraire 70 (1 April 1969): 22-23.

Duhamel, Roger. "Voulez-vous des romans?" L'Action universitaire 18.1 (Oct. 1951): 82-84.

Flower, J. E. *Roger Vailland, The Man and his Masks*. London: Hodder and Stoughton, 1975.
---. "Roger Vailland's *325,000 francs*." *Modern Languages* 53 (1972): 63-71.
---. "Three Party Writers: André Stil, Roger Vailland, Pierre Courtade." *Literature and the Left in France*. Totowa (New Jersey): Barnes & Noble, 1983. 151-181.
Freustié, Jean. "Vailland pêche en eau froide." *France-Observateur* 23 (April 1964): 14.
Gaddis-Rose, Marilyn. Rev. of *La Truite*. *French Review* 40.1 (Oct. 1966): 171-72.
Georgin, René. "Comment écrit Roger Vailland contre les lois grammaticales." *Arts* 4-10 Dec. 1957: 2.
Georis, Michel. "Roger Vailland entre la fête et la loi." *Revue de Paris* 75 (Jan. 1968): 97-103.
Gilbert-Lecomte, Roger. "Correspondance à Roger Vailland." *NRF* 17 (Nov. 1969): 695-701.
Guth, Paul. "L'Oiseau Vailland." *Quarante contre un*. Paris: Corrêa, 1947. 285-89.
Hoog, Armand. "Portrait d'une demi-génération." *La Nef* 3.16 (March 1946): 114-17.
Kanters, Robert. "Entre l'Homme et l'Oeuvre." *Revue de Paris* 4 (April 1969): 131-33.
---. "Roger Vailland." *Preuves* 59 (Jan. 1956): 83.
Kast, Pierre. "Roger Vailland vu par Pierre Kast." *Magazine littéraire* 8 (June 1967): 17-18.
Kneller, J. W. Rev. of *La Fête*. *French Review* 34.5 (April 1961): 499-500.
Lalou, René. "La Fête." *Annales* 67.118 (Aug. 1960): 11-12.
---. "La Loi." *Annales* 64.83 (Sept. 1957).
---. "Roger Vailland." *Revue de Paris* 64 (Aug. 1957): 159-60.
Lartigue, Jean. "Roger Vailland, *Beau Masque*." *Cahier du Sud* 41.327 (Feb. 1955): 337.
Laufer, Roger. "Le Héros tragique dans les romans de Roger Vailland." *AUMLA* 22 (1964): 221-32.
Lemarchand, Jacques. "Roger Vailland." *Livres de France* Dec. 1959: 2-3.
Leterrier, François. "Un Livre de Qualité." *La Nef* 14.9 (Sept. 1957): 37-39.
Mathias, Pierre. Rev. of *La Loi*. *Cahiers du Sud* 44.344 (Jan. 1958): 150.
Matignon, Renaud. "*La Loi* de Roger Vailland." *Arts* 4-10 Dec. 1957: 2.
Mauvais, Yves. "L'Écriture en défaut." *Littérature* 33 (1979): 75-85.
Michel, Marc. "Le Loup, Notes sur un animal mythique." *NRF* 12.140 (1 Aug. 1964): 370-381.
Mithois, Marcel. "Les Secrets de l'écrivain Roger Vailland." *Réalités* 218 (March 1964): 81-88.
Nott, David, ed. *325.000 francs*. London: English Universities Press, 1975.
Nourissier, François. "François Nourissier n'aime pas les 'Liaisons Vadim-Vailland' et le prouve." *La Nef* 16.31 (Oct. 1959): 80-83.
---. "Roger Vailland n'est pas immortel." *Nouvelles littéraires* 20 May 1965: 3.
Parinaud, André. "Roger Vailland: 'J'ai un Don Juan moderne à offrir à Paris.'" *Arts* 4-10 Dec. 1957: 1,4.
Pérol, Jean. "À la Recherche de l'héroïsme, de la tendresse et de la licornéité: Roger Vailland." *NRF* 17 (April 1969): 576-85.
Petr, Christian. "Le Discours du roman réaliste: *325.000 francs* de Roger Vailland." *French Review* 57.2 (1983): 194-202.

Picard Michel. Libertinage et tragique dans l'oeuvre de Roger Vailland. Paris: Hachette, 1972.
---. "On n'est pas sorti de l'auberge." Littérature 6 (May 1972): 20-32.
---. "Roger Vailland et Le Grand Jeu." Revue d'histoire littéraire de la France 4 (1979): 613-622.
---. "Le Thème des mères chez Roger Vailland." Revue d'histoire littéraire de la France 71 (1971): 638-61.
Piroué, Georges. "L'Univers romanesque de Roger Vailland." Comprendre 19 (1958): 258-60.
Pritchett, V. S. Rev. of La Loi. New Statesman 54.1382 (7 Sept. 1957): 281.
Recanati, Jean. Esquisse pour la psychanalyse d'un libertin, Roger Vailland. Paris: Buchet-Chastel, 1971.
Rolland, J. F. "Roger Vailland, mon ami." Magazine littéraire 8 (June 1967): 15-17.
Roy, Claude. "Esquisse d'une description critique de Roger Vailland." Les Temps Modernes Dec. 1957: 1071-98.
---. "Profil gauche de Roger Vailland." La Quinzaine littéraire 22 (15 Feb. 1967): 12-13.
---. "Roger Vailland par l'un des treize." Nous. Essai d'autobiographie. Paris: Gallimard, 1972. 217-63.
Sabord, Noel. "Les Mauvais Coups." Nouvelles littéraires 3 Feb. 1949: 3.
Senart, Philippe. "La Littérature communiste: Foi et libertinage." Arts 7 March 1957: 2.
Sicard, Alain. "Réflexions sur l'oeuvre de Roger Vailland." Nouvelle critique 172 (Feb. 1966): 19-41.
Tavernier, René. "La Liberté par le libertinage." Preuves 81 (Nov. 1957): 85-86.
Thiébaut, Marcel. "Les Prix." Revue de Paris 65 (Jan. 1958): 170-71.
---. "Roger Vailland." Revue de Paris 55 (Dec. 1948): 152-53.
Tracy, H. Rev. of The Law. The Listener 60.1534 (21 Aug. 1958): 279.
Tusseau, Jean-Pierre. Roger Vailland: Un écrivain au service du peuple. Paris: Nouvelles Éditions Debresse, 1976.
Vailland, Elisabeth. "Elisabeth Vailland raconte." Magazine littéraire 8 (June 1967): 11-15.
Vandromme, Pol. "L'Apologiste du libertinage." La Droite buissonnière. Paris: Sept Couleurs, 1960. Chap. 10.
Verthuy, Mair. "Vision du monde, vision des femmes dans trois romans de Roger Vailland." Signum (Royal Military College of Canada) 3 (1982): 535-60.
Williams, Orlo. "Aspects of French Resistance." The National Review 766 (Dec. 1946): 517-22.

Peter N. Pedroni

Existance as Theme in Carlo Cassola's Fiction

American University Studies:
Series II, Romance Languages and Literature. Vol. 31
ISBN 0-8204-0236-2 192 pp. hardback US $ 26.65

Despite his early reputation as a neorealist, Cassola's themes were existential and his purpose was always to express existential emotions – the feeling of awe the contemplation of the importance of the opposite sex as a catalyst to active participation in life, the mysterious ways in which a life's destiny is determined, the irrevocable passing of time with its inherent sense of loss, the fundamental sadness caused by the necessity of death, and joy in the acceptance of existence as an absolute value in itself. The material that he used to express these emotions ranges from everyday life in small town Italy to action-filled combat scenes based on his own experiences as a partisan fighter during World War II.

Cassola's fiction offers the reader an unusally clear perspective of the complexities of contemporary Italian society and of the relationship of the individual to that society.

Lucy L. Melbourne

Double Heart : Explicit and Implicit Texts in Bellow, Camus and Kafka

American University Studies:
Series III: Comporative Literature. Vol. 21
ISBN 0-8204-0264-8 252 pp. approx. US $ 31.90

What distinguishes fiction from non-fiction in first-person narratives? What is the difference between a novel and autobiography? What makes a first-person narrative a literary work of art? If fiction is a self-contained meaning structure, what frame of reference can we use to tell if the narrator is "lying?" Using a phenomenological approach to these questions basic to both literary theory and practical criticism, Dr. Melbourne develops a model of the unreliable first-person narrative. By applying it to three challenging works, Saul Bellow's *Dangling Man,* Albert Camus's *La Chute,* and Franz Kafka's *"Ein Landarzt,"* she shows us how to read "between the lines" to discover the implicit text structuring first-person narratives into literary works of art.

PETER LANG PUBLISHING, INC.
62 West 45th Street
USA - New York, NY 10036

Neal Storrs

LIQUID

A Source of Meaning and Structure in Claude Simon's *La Bataille de Pharsale*

American University Studies:
Series II, Romance Languages and Literature. Vol. 4.
ISBN 0-8204-0021-1 151 pp. paperback US $ 16.85

Applying his own adaptation of structuralist criticism, the author seeks out the modes of meaning in one of most difficult of the French *romans experimentaux*. Mr. Storrs identifies liquid-related material from the realms of description, phonology, and narration, and shows how the complicated patterns of association between those elements illuminate the adventures of the novel's two central protagonists and reveal the creative principle which underpins *La Bataille de Pharsale.*

Dean Vasil

The Ethical Pragmatism of Albert Camus

Two Studies in the History of Ideas

American University Studies:
Series II: Romance Languages and Literature. Vol. 18
ISBN 0-8204-0166-8 XVI + 152 pp. hardback US $ 21.85

In what, since the age of its Enlightenment, the West has perceived to be an absurd universe, it has had continually to choose between two ways of life as consequences of that perception and of the movement which gave it rise: these are the way of ethics and the way of modern historicist ideology, the way of a moral imperative without God and that of the will to become God in His place. The first is illogical, but the second is irrational, la «prédication de la surhumanité», as Camus says, «aboutissant à la fabrication méthodique des sous-hommes.» The way of ethics or of man as an end in himself is the way of Camus as well, and one the reflection of whose origins and *raison d'être* in his own thought is the subject of the two studies in the present essay.

PETER LANG PUBLISHING, INC.
62 West 45th Street
USA - New York, NY 10036